EP Sport Series

ep EP PUBLISHING LIMITED

epsport

volleyball

Barrie MacGregor

Cover picture: veteran Japanese setter and captain, Nekoda (2), places the ball out of reach of the Russian blockers at the Montreal Olympics, photographed by Wardener, Norway.

Frontispiece, courtesy of *Sandwell Evening Mail,* shows the England team putting away the final point against Scotland at Sandwell, January 1977.

The sequence, training and British Caledonian Cup photographs are by Jim Cockayne. The other photographs are by the author.

ISBN 0 7158 0568 1

Published 1977 by EP Publishing Ltd., East Ardsley, Wakefield, West Yorkshire

Reprinted 1981

Text set in 11/12 pt Monophoto Univers, printed by photolithography by G. Beard & Son, Brighton, Sussex, and bound in Great Britain by Seawhite Ltd., Brighton, Sussex.

Contents

Introduction

William G. Morgan invented the game of volleyball in 1896 when he was the physical training instructor at the YMCA in Holyoke, Massachusetts. He found that basketball was too strenuous an activity for his overweight businessmen's keep-fit class and introduced this new game to help improve fitness for these middle-aged gentlemen. He originally stretched a tennis net across the gymnasium at a height of about 6 ft (2 m) and used the bladder of a basketball to be passed back and forth over the net. As the game caught on locally a sporting goods manufacturer produced a ball which was of similar construction to a soccer ball but lighter, and the specifications laid down then have stayed with the game to the present.

The game was later demonstrated at Springfield College where Morgan had received his training, and one of the professors called it 'volleyball'. Since that time volleyball has been spread throughout the world by the YMCA and the American armed forces, to the extent that it is now one of the most popular sports in the world.

Volleyball has taken various forms and has been developed in a lot of different ways. In its native United States the game is played on a recreational level by everyone, and there are some pockets of intense enthusiasm and high-calibre play. The sport is accepted as part of the competitive programme in schools, colleges, universities and YMCAs, and recently a professional league has been started in the West. Beach volleyball, where two-man teams play each other in the California sun, attracts huge crowds of spectators and sometimes prize money as well. In Japan volleyball has gained tremendous popularity but in early days was played as a nine-man game with players being allowed to attack from all positions, making for a lot of interesting and varied play. Volleyball is certainly one of the major sports in Japan and is very popular as a spectator activity as well. Volleyball received its major development as a power game in Eastern Europe, and this section of the world still dominates the game. Much of the volleyball originally played in Eastern European countries, even championships, was on outdoor courts. Top club teams in Japan and Western Europe are sponsored by factories whereas East European top teams come from the military, universities or sports clubs.

At the present time Europe is the strongest zone in the world for top-class volleyball. In the Montreal Olympics eight out of the eighteen teams which qualified came from Europe. At the 1974 World Championships in Mexico eight of the top twelve teams in the men's competition were from Europe and five of the top twelve teams in the women's event were from this zone as well. In the Asian zone Japan's men and women are constantly in the top echelon of national teams. Even those who are not volleyball enthusiasts will remember the startling training techniques used to develop the Japanese women's team for the Olympics in Tokyo in 1964. The Japanese, because they lack tall players when compared with European teams, have devised a highly demanding style of play involving fast attacking shots and deception. At the Montreal Olympics the emergence of Cuba was obvious as they defeated the Japanese men for the bronze medal with their high-flying and dynamically exciting play.

Volleyball came into Britain from two sources as a result of the Second World War. American armed services personnel played volleyball as part of their recreation programme, thus giving the game some impetus. Expatriot East Europeans who played in their newly formed social clubs provided in Britain a quality of game that would not have been available otherwise. It is only recently that the Polish clubs have not been in the top rankings of the United Kingdom national leagues, but a brief look at a sample of the team rosters will show that the influence is still being felt.

The Amateur Volleyball Association of Great Britain was formed in 1955 and initially governed all the volleyball activity in Britain. In the late 1960s with the emergence of greater activity in Scotland a separate association was formed and was affiliated to the IVBF (International Volleyball Federation). The English Volleyball Association was formed at the same time. Until recently British volleyball has been played and developed mostly in England and Scotland. A Northern Ireland Volleyball Association has been functioning for some years and in 1976 the Welsh Volleyball Association was formed. Both England and Scotland have active executive committees backed up by full-time administrative staff.

Development and promotion work is carried out in coaching, competitions, officiating, national teams and information services. Both these associations run national leagues, as well as men's and women's national teams. Normally the competitive season for volleyball in Britain runs from October through to April. Some tournaments are usually staged outside this period to provide additional friendly competition.

The national teams from England and Scotland compete primarily within Western Europe and on a limited basis. Neither country is yet on a par with the stronger West European countries but with the consistent improvement in domestic competitions, coaching development and international experience the results continue to get better. The popularity of volleyball is international and incontestable. There are 130 countries affiliated to the IVBF and it has one of the highest numbers of registered participants. Although less popular in Britain than in many other countries the game has such a basic appeal that most who come into contact with it play enthusiastically or become ardent spectators. The idea of the game itself is very basic and the object is easily recognised by people watching or playing for the first time. Volleyball can be played and enjoyed at any level of skill. With the new methods of introducing the game (see EVA Notes for Teachers) a competitive and enjoyable situation can be developed very easily and quickly with young and old beginners alike. As the player's skill, commitment and enthusiasm increases so he or she can scale the ladder of progress by competing in higher and higher leagues. As these factors diminish and age increases the individual can come back down the ladder and take part at the level at which he feels most comfortable. In this way volleyball is a social skill as well as a physical one. The top-class game, however,

has tremendous demands, requiring physical prowess, mental toughness and great tactical knowledge and ability. Anyone watching the Olympic finals could testify to this. Because of these demands and the scope for development in volleyball many are attracted to the game and remain involved for many years.

It is assumed that people reading this book already have a basic knowledge of the game of volleyball, have probably played it at club level and wish to learn more about how to play the game and perhaps become involved in coaching. This book is aimed at the individual player who wishes to learn more about the performance of his skills, the basic tactics of the game and ways of improving his play. The book will also be useful for beginning coaches who are looking for some ideas on training methods and development for either the club or school team. Volleyball is essentially a team sport and though players can increase

their skill level and fitness individually, it is through working together in a team that personal performance is put in context.

The chapter on systems of play is essential reading for both coaches and players. An individual who has the basic skills of the game but cannot put himself in the right place on court will have great difficulty in playing volleyball properly or successfully. The systems described in this book are basic, but other more complex systems evolve from what is described here. Being aware of the systems of offence and defence will allow players to play the game with greater intelligence. For players or coaches who wish for greater knowledge there is a bibliography on page 114.

Skills

Just as individual notes make up a symphony, the individual skills of volleyball make up the game; and just as one false note in a piece of music mars the whole composition, one action inefficiently carried out in volleyball can ruin the whole match. For this reason — and, especially, early in their development — players must develop all the skills to play the game of volleyball successfully. There is often a great desire to take the tall players and emphasise their attacking ability and at the same time turn the smaller players into setters; if this is the case the players' development and enjoyment at later stages are hindered. Some may be surprised to see movement listed and described here as a skill while others may wonder why it was left to the last. There has been a tendency among some coaches to teach skills in isolation with little or no gross body movement involved. Body movement is the important ingredient that ties all the game skills together, and it is an error to teach the

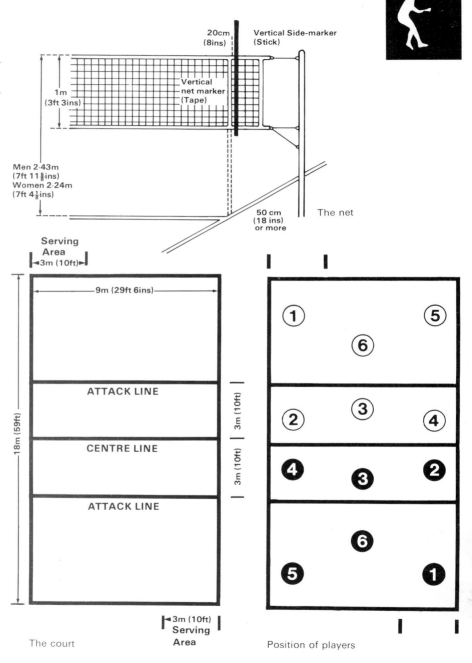

20cm (8ins)

Vertical Side-marker (Stick)

Vertical net marker (Tape)

1m (3ft 3ins)

Men 2·43m (7ft 11⅝ins)
Women 2·24m (7ft 4⅛ins)

50 cm (18 ins) or more

The net

Serving Area
3m (10ft)

9m (29ft 6ins)

18m (59ft)

ATTACK LINE

3m (10ft)

CENTRE LINE

3m (10ft)

ATTACK LINE

3m (10ft) Serving Area

The court

① ⑤
⑥
② ③ ④
❹ ❸ ❷
❻
❺ ❶

Position of players

skills without some element of movement included even in the early stages. Developing the ability to move, range of movement, range of motion and knowledge of where and when to move are integral parts of the game of volleyball. The manner in which the skills are described and developed is the preference of this author. With the combination of the written description and the accompanying photographs a player should be able to obtain an accurate concept of the method of performing a skill and the coach should be better prepared to teach. The descriptions here are the basic, orthodox ways the skills are performed and beginning players should be wary of unusual techniques used by top-class players regardless of the success they achieve. It is on a foundation of orthodox skills that the more sophisticated movements will be developed. The order in which the skills are listed here is the order in which this author would introduce them, but again

others may choose a different sequence. It must be stressed that successful play results from a strong basis of skills combined with good movement.

The Volley

The volley or the two-handed overhead pass is the basic

method of playing the ball in volleyball. In this skill once the body is in the proper position in relation to the ball the player goes through the following sequence of movements:

1. His hands are brought to a position between shoulder and ear level with the fingers outstretched.

2. He then bends at the knees

Hand position for the volley

and hips going into a slight crouching position. The depth of the crouch will vary with the amount of force he wishes to apply to the ball in the volley.
3. When the ball is in a position close to the forehead — i.e. 4–6 in. (100–150 mm) — the player accelerates his hands from the position described above so that he contacts the ball with his fingers just in front of his forehead. He continues to extend to the full distance possible and the ball is released from the hands.
4. When the ball comes in contact with the fingertips the body is moving forward due to muscle activity in the legs and arms, but the wrists are held semi-relaxed so that the hands bend backwards involuntarily with the initial contact. The hands are fully extended at the wrists as the ball is released, however.
A lot of the power going into passing the ball comes from the leg muscles whereas the control comes from the arms

Movements for the volley

(a)

(b)

(c)

(d)

11

and wrists. For shorter passes, particularly in setting, the legs come much less into play, but all players should learn to volley the ball for distance and accuracy.

Some additional teaching points involved in preparing to volley and in the performance of the skill follow:

■ move into position early so that the ball will land on the player's forehead if it were not volleyed;

■ do not leave the floor during the volley;

■ face the direction in which the ball is to be passed;

■ the feet should be firmly planted prior to extension and should be one in front of the other;

■ extension should be complete with the hands starting close to the shoulders and finishing with the final flexion of the wrists just as the ball is released from the hands. The hands will actually be in contact with the ball for as much as 10–14 in. (250–350 mm) during the volley;

■ the ball is contacted with the thumbs and fingerprints, and not with the palms of the hands.

Canadian setter prepared for volley

The Dig

The dig, sometimes called the 'bump', is the two-hand underhand pass and is the second most commonly used pass in volleyball. It is used primarily for receiving serve and attacks from the opposition. The dig is used because in many cases handling errors would result if the volley was used, and also because the ball is too close to the floor to get in a proper position for the overhead pass to be used. There is a tendency for some players to use the dig too much and in cases where they could in fact use a volley. This is usually due to slow movement into position or lack of confidence in the volleying skill. The following are the steps involved in performing the dig:

1. The player moves into a position so that the ball will be received between shoulders and knees and he is facing the direction in which he intends to pass the ball. If the player intends to pass the ball to the right then the left foot should be forward and vice versa.

2. The knees should be bent, the depth depending on how low the ball to be played is going to be, and the arms should be extended in front of the body.

3. The hands are held together in the manner illustrated in the photograph below, with the wrists bent down, keeping the arms straight at the elbows.

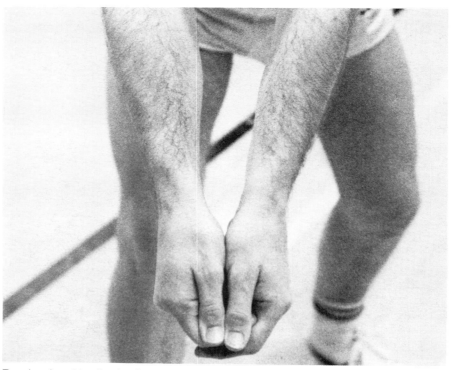

Two-hand position for the dig

(a)

(b)

(c)

(d)

4. As the ball comes in contact with the fleshy part of the lower arms the player must be in such a position that the ball will rebound off in the desired direction. In most cases the player is attempting to absorb energy from the ball rather than impart it so that very little movement is required. The motion used is more of a 'steering' movement than an arm swing with most of the guidance coming from the legs.

The height necessary for the ball to go in the air will be dictated by the type of system the team is playing and the level of skill acquired in directing the ball. It is advisable in the early stages for players to pass the ball high in the air, allowing team-mates greater opportunity to get under it for the next play in the sequence.

Digging sequence

Russian back-court player receives Brazil's smash with a dig

The Service

The service is the method by which the ball is put into play at the beginning of each rally and for this reason it is a very important skill. Because only the team serving scores points in volleyball, it is critical that a player serve well, using the following order of priorities in his serving.

1. First of all the ball must go into the opponents' court with regularity. Players must use a type of service through which they can serve into court a minimum of 90 per cent of the time.
2. Players must learn to direct the ball to various parts of the opponents' court towards areas of weakness but still abiding by the first priority.
3. The next priority is power, lessening the amount of time that the opposition have in preparing to receive the ball from service.
4. Next the player must learn to make the ball move in some fashion while it passes through the air towards the opposition.

This can be accomplished by putting either a lot of spin on the ball or practically none at all. If a lot of top-spin is put on the ball it will have a tendency to drop quickly in front of the players receiving serve. If the ball is struck with enough force and has very little spin it will 'float' as it approaches the receivers. A ball that floats on service moves in the air unpredictably in any plane, often not allowing the player receiving the ball time enough to react and perform the skill properly. At top levels of play this is the serve used the majority of the time.

For beginning players it cannot be emphasised too much that the service must go into court and be 'kept at' the opposition. As players advance the service becomes the first offensive play of a rally and should be regarded as such.

Underhand Service

The first type of serve to learn and probably the easiest is the underhand service; in this the ball is tossed only slightly in the air and is hit about waist high by the player's dominant hand. The ball may be struck with a closed fist or with an open hand, there being more control with the latter and greater force imparted by the former. As the arm of the hand used to strike the ball moves like a pendulum and the toss is not particularly high, the skill demands of this service are not great. Players should keep the feet firmly placed on the floor, with the left foot slightly in front of the right in the case of a right-handed player.

(a)

(b)

Underhand service

(c)

Tennis Service

The overhand tennis serve is usually the first overhand service taught. The ball is tossed overhead, slightly in front of the shoulder of the arm that is to be used in hitting the ball. As the ball is tossed the server draws his arm back much as though he was throwing a stone and then swings it forward in time to hit the ball when his arm is fully extended. The main advantage of the overhand service is that the ball is hit at a point higher in the air than in the underhand so that the force applied to it can be greater. This means that the ball should reach the opposition more quickly than it would do if it were served underhand, leaving the receiving team less time to react.

Tennis service   (a)   (b)

Spinning the Ball

To apply spin the ball must be contacted with a loose wrist: the heel of the hand contacts the ball first and the wrist snaps through so that the palm of the hand and fingers contact the ball just after. This will put op-spin on the ball and cause t to drop more quickly in its flight. It is easier to carry out his contact if the ball is tossed o a point just slightly behind he shoulder of the hitting hand.

Float

To make the ball 'float' as it passes through the air it should be contacted with force but must have virtually no spin on it as it travels. The ball will hen move off its path of flight at times and directions that are mpossible to predict by either the server or the receiver. This s by far the most difficult service to receive, but considerable practice is equired to hit the ball so it has no spin and is travelling at the ight velocity to float.

Roundhouse or Windmill Service

Although it looks rather devastating, the roundhouse service is a relatively easy method of putting the ball into play and at intermediate levels of competition can be quite effective. In this serve the ball crosses the net with a great deal of force and a lot of top-spin so that it has a tendency to 'drop' at the players' feet if they are not experienced enough to judge its flight path. The player stands with his side towards the net and throws the ball in the air several feet over his right (hitting) shoulder. He contacts the ball with a cupped hand over the shoulder and follows through forward towards the net. The direction of the ball will be pointed out by the left shoulder. To alter the direction the foot position should be changed accordingly.

The Smash

The smash, spike or attack is the principal offensive weapon in the game of volleyball and is one of the major attractions for spectators and players alike. The main idea is to have the ball in the air above and close to the net so that an attack player may jump and hit the ball with force down into the opponents' court. The object of the skill is to hit the ball in a direction that will avoid any defensive (blocking) players near the net on the opposition's side and with enough velocity to make it difficult for the back-court players to move in time to make contact or, if contact is made, to control the pass. The smash is a very difficult skill because the ball is moving, the player has to jump in the air, he must hit the ball over one obstacle, around another and still keep the ball within the confines of the 29 ft 6 in (9 m) square volleyball court. For explanation and teaching the skill can best be divided into three parts: (i) the approach, (ii) the jump or take-off and (iii) the smash phase.

Roundhouse floating service

(a)

(b)

(c)

(d)

(e)

Japanese women's captain using roundhouse floater in Montreal

The main purpose of the approach run is to assist the attacker in 'gathering' himself for the jump in much the same way as a high jumper. However, because it is against the rules to contact the net there must be as little forward movement as possible during the period of time in the air, so there is a fair emphasis on control during the approach phase. We must assume that the setter will be placing the ball in the air about 1–2 ft (0·3–0·6 m) from the net and in front of the attack player. The smasher will be preparing to attack from a position about 10–13 ft (3–4 m) from the net and will not move until he sees the initial flight of the ball as it leaves the hands of the setter. In some cases players will leave on their approach run before the ball leaves the setter's hands, making it impossible to judge the exact location of the set.

The simplest approach to use is one involving only three steps. Once the attacker sees the initial flight of the ball he uses

The smash approach

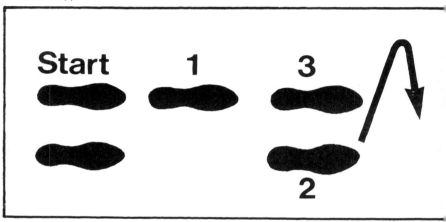

his first step to make a minor adjustment in relation to where he will ultimately hit the ball. The second step may allow for a further adjustment but will primarily be used to gain momentum for his jump. In the third step the foot will be brought up next to the front foot, and it will be from this platform that the player performs his jump. The last two foot-plants will be carried out with the heels hitting first so that the smasher can absorb some of his forward momentum and put his large leg muscles into stretch, thus adding to the

jumping force. The player will also be leaning slightly backwards at this point better to absorb his forward momentum.

After the heel plant by both feet is accomplished the player will rock forward on to his toes or the balls of his feet, putting his calf muscles in stretch as well. At the same time his arms are swung behind him. This is the end of the approach, and if this part of the attack is carried out correctly in relation to the ball that has been set, the remainder of the skill is relatively easy. However, if this

(a)

(b)

(c)

(d)

(e)

(f)

part of the skill is not done in the right way there will have to be compensating moves introduced in either or both of the jump or the attack phases that will diminish the overall effectiveness of the skill.

The jump phase of the attack is purely one of explosive muscular contraction with the player's centre of gravity being propelled vertically as high in the air as possible. It is essential that a player jumps as high as possible no matter what his height. The higher in the air he can attack the ball the better chance he will have of going over the net or even the top of the block. Also, the longer the attacker has his hand above the net the greater his margin for error if he has mistimed his approach. The jump is enhanced greatly by co-ordinated swinging of the arms upward from a position behind the body. This also puts the attacking arm in the correct position in preparation for the smash phase. So, after the jump, the player should be high in the air, facing the net about 2 ft (0·6 m) from the net, with his back arched and his attacking hand behind his head and all the muscles that go into the attacking motion in stretch. Ideally the smasher should hit the ball at the peak of his jump where he appears to stop in mid-air. When the attacker is approaching this point in the air he swings his arm forward using the muscles of his abdomen, chest and arm which have already been tensed by stretching. When the hand comes in contact with the ball, the heel of the hand touches first then the cupped hand follows through quickly not so much by muscular contraction but due to the fact that it is relaxed at the wrist. This is the same action that was used to put top-spin on the ball in the tennis service. Snapping the wrist over like this will add force to the ball and also apply top-spin, causing the ball to curve in a downward direction in its flight. The contact with the ball is the summation of the movements imparted on the hand by trunk, chest, upper arm, lower arm and the hand itself. Done correctly by top-class players, the ball can be made to move at speeds up to 100 ft (30 m) per second, not allowing players in the back court time enough to react once the ball has been hit.

As indicated earlier, this skill is a very difficult one; what has been explained here is the basic skill. There are an infinite number of variations to consider such as hitting around the block, turning the body whilst in the air, moving sideways after the jump, etc. It is important that players learn the basic skill first and that they learn to increase both their power and accuracy effectively and in a complementary manner. It is also important to learn the three phases of the skill properly or it will never be carried out correctly or at advanced levels. If the approach is wrong, or the jump is not carried out correctly a tall player may still be able to smash, but he would be much more effective if he learned the skill properly.

Russian women attack against Japan in Olympic final

Cuba hits off Canadian block

Cuban attacker places tactical ball around Canadian block

The Tip

The tip or tactical ball is a shot that is performed after faking an attack. That is, a player has been set, comes in to attack, jumps high in the air and at the last instant, rather than hitting the ball with force downwards into the court, he either tips it gently over the top of the block or passes it to the back corner of the court. This skill is usually carried out with the finger tips of one hand or with a volley. The critical aspect of this skill is that it should look like an attack up until the last instant. All too often players will give away that they are about to tip the ball so that the defence is ready. Also — do not tip only when in trouble. There is a tendency for attackers to use a tip on occasions when for some reason they cannot hit the ball with force. The best and most effective time to use a tactical ball is when everyone on the opposition is expecting the attacker to smash and have prepared themselves accordingly.

Russian team mounts three-man block in the middle

The Block

The block is the first line of defence and on the strength of a team's block may depend the type of defensive tactics the team will use to achieve the most success. It is also imperative that players realise that blocking is a team effort in at least two ways. First of all,

only on rare occasions does a player in the front court block by himself; so to be an effective block the two, or sometimes three, players involved must work together to form one block of substance rather than two or three different blocks which are ineffective. The other team aspect involves the rest of the

players not taking part in the block. They must know what the block is trying to do so that they can adjust the back-court play accordingly. There will be more on this in the chapter on defence (see pages 67–71). When the ball passes over the net into the opponents' court from service or some other play, the three front-court

Cuban women block out Canadian attacker

players should be standing close to the net with the centre player in the middle of the net and the two other front-court players about 8 ft (2·5 m) from him on either side. The initial stage of learning where to block requires the blockers to watch where the ball is set once it leaves the setter's hands. From the first part of the ball flight the front-court players should be able to predict where the ball will be attacked and how much time the block has in which to prepare. The other cue as to where to set the block comes from the player who is on attack. The blockers, once they are aware of the opponent who is going to attack the ball, must observe his approach to determine (i) the point at

England women putting up strong block at Spring Cup in Denmark, 1977

Cuban smasher having an easy hit against a Japanese one-man block

which he will actually attack the ball, and (ii) the angle through which he will most likely attack. In assuming that the block will involve only two of the front-court players, i.e. the middle player and one of the side players, one of these will determine where the block is to be placed and the other will make an adjustment to comply with this decision. In some systems the centre blocker makes the decision while in other teams it is the player on the side who decides where the block should be located. It is critical that the block be formed as a single unit so that the ball cannot be smashed through it.

Players moving in the front court to prepare for the block need only move laterally, and

Ryskla, three times medal winner in Olympic volleyball, smashes for the Russian ladies' team against a Japanese block

for this reason use a shuffle step. This prevents the players from coming into contact with the net as they move along it and also puts them in the correct position for take-off on the block. The actual jumping technique is different from that used in the smash, as the players are jumping from a position that is almost stationary and they are limited by the amount of arm movement that can be used because of the close proximity of the net. The arms are not swung forward as in the smash jump; rather, they are thrust into the air giving a small added momentum to the jump. Normally players will not be able to jump as high on the block as they can in a smash due to the lack of build-up in momentum. When the players jump they should endeavour to have the outside hand of the outside blocker opposite the attacking arm of the opponent. This is a rule of thumb only and need not apply at higher levels of play. This positioning of the block should protect the

greater portion of the court on the diagonal or cross-court side and leave the attack player with a difficult line shot. At higher levels of play much more thinking and tactical play goes into setting the block. The players in the block, in defending against a normal attack coming from 2–3 ft (0·6–0·9 m) away from the net, should jump just after the attack player has jumped and not at the same time. The farther away from the net the ball is to be attacked, the later the blockers jump. The classic style for the block is to jump leading with the hands which go up and over the net and in over the opponents' court. The blockers are allowed to contact the ball over the opponents' court after the attack is completed and to their obvious advantage. The advantage being (i) if the ball contacts the block it will land in the attacker's court, and (ii) the closer the block is to the ball the less angle the attack player has available to him through which to hit. Once the blockers

reach the peak of their jump and begin to fall, they must be sure to withdraw their hands from the opponents' court and avoid contacting the net. Contact with the net at this stage nullifies any success achieved on the block. The blocker's job is not completed once he is on his way back to the floor. Although his tasks as a blocker are finished he must now react to what has happened during the opponents' attack. If the block has been successful and the ball has landed on the opponents' court then the play is over and the game continues with the blocker's team serving. If the block has been only semi-successful and the opponents are back on the attack the blocker gets back to the ready position described earlier and prepares for another block. If the ball has hit the block as it is coming down on the blocker's side of the net then the blocker must be prepared to play the ball close to the floor and in front of him. This will require a quick

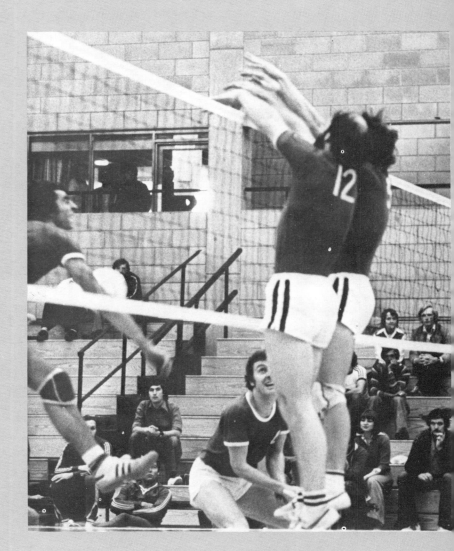

Scottish men's team sends the ball back
at Luxembourg with an attacking block

underhand shot with the fist avoiding a carry.

If the ball has been hit off the block or around the block and into the blocker's court he must determine the location of the ball and whether or not he will be required to play it again. This means that as a player lands from the block he must turn and face the side of the court to which the ball travelled. He can best accomplish this by landing on the foot opposite to the side to which the ball has gone. That is, if the ball has passed a blocker on his left hand, he should land initially on his right foot and take a short step with his left foot towards the back court. This will put him in the correct position to make the next play which may be required immediately. With the alteration of the rules of the IVBF congress in Montreal a team is now allowed three more hits after the ball is contacted by the block. This may lend new importance to the technique of defensive blocking. Normally

this method of blocking is used by players who cannot get high in the air for the block. Rather than extending the arms and hands over the net these players go for maximum height and slant their hands backwards so that any ball hitting their hands will return into their own court and will be available for further play. In the pre-Montreal rules this rarely led to an attack, but with the inception of the additional hit following the block this method of blocking may become more effective and more prevalent as a deliberate ploy.

One-Handed Dig

There is a priority in the ways a player should attempt to play a ball; beginning with the volley, followed by the two-handed dig and then followed by the one-handed dig. At times when the ball is moving too quickly for the player to make the necessary body adjustments to play the ball by either the volley or the dig he will have to reach out with one hand and keep the ball in play. The ball is contacted with either the fist or the lower part of the forearm. The important point to remember is that the forearm must be turned so that the palm of the hand would be facing forward if the hand were open. Since the majority of balls played in this manner will be coming towards the player with some force the main effort is to assure that the ball does not 'get past' the defender and that it will be playable by another member of the team. If the arm is held so that the palm of the hand would be flat, the ball would probably skid

Korean lady player makes emergency play defending against a Russian smash

off the arm and out the back or side of the court.

The Roll and Dive

The roll and the dive are probably the most spectacular defensive plays in volleyball in the same way in which the smash is the most spectacular on offence. For this reason some coaches mistakenly spend time on teaching these skills when their players have not come close to mastering the volley, dig and serve. The two defensive skills to be described here are sophisticated techniques, and though they should be included in the instruction at club level this should not be to the detriment of learning the basic skills to a high degree.

The Roll

The roll is simply an extension of the one-handed dig to the side, in which the player extends his body farther than his immediate reach and uses a rolling technique to avoid injury to himself and assist in recovering for the next play. The object of using this skill is to recover a ball that is close to the floor and some distance away from the player to the side of his body. A good player should be able to retrieve a ball that is 8–10 ft (2·5–3 m) away by means of one step and a well-executed roll.

Initially, since the player is on defence he should be in a low position. The first stage of the skill is a step to the side in the direction of the ball with the arm extended in the same manner as in the one-handed dig. Once the foot is placed on the floor in the new position the heel should be turned in the direction of the ball. In this way the player's centre of gravity is put closer to the floor and he will roll on to his buttocks with little impact, since that part of his body is now only centimetres away from the floor. It is at this stage that the player should be ready to play the ball, but this will vary depending on how far away the ball is. After he plays the ball in the same way as in the one-handed dig, his forearm contacts the floor, absorbing some of the force of the fall, and is followed by the upper arm and shoulder. If the player is playing a ball to his right his roll will be over his right shoulder and left hip, so that he will return to his feet facing the net.

Because this is an emergency technique it is not always performed in the orthodox way and the point of contact with the ball is not always the same. It is important to teach players how far they can actually go to reach a ball in an emergency and how to reach laterally without causing injury. Even if the roll itself cannot be completed because the player has reached too far to roll he will have done so with a small chance of hurting himself if he has practised this technique.

Roll sequence

(a)

(b)

(c)

d)

(e)

(f)

The Dive

The dive is used to recover a ball that is falling close to the floor some distance in front of a defending player. Probably the most common time to use this particular skill is when an attack player has tipped over the block and the defender is in the back court too far away to get in to volley or dig the ball. On this occasion he will have to dive, retrieve the ball with the back of his hand and recover without injury to himself. It is assumed that since the player is in a defensive position he will be low, with his centre of gravity fairly close to the floor. Once he sees that the ball is falling into court he will use primarily his leg muscles along with some assistance from arm swing to cover the distance between himself and ball.

He should contact the ball with the back of the hand closest to the side on which the ball is located. The fingers of the hand are held closely together and curved backwards, forming

Dive sequence

(a)

a fairly hard surface off which to play the ball. Once the ball has been played — and the object here is to keep it in play — the player must quickly be prepared to absorb the force of his body as it accelerates towards the floor. This is carried out by landing on the hands with the arms outstretched in a press-up position. As the hands touch the floor and the force of the body is felt the muscles of the arms gently bring the body to the

floor. There may still be some force left to absorb and this is done by sliding along the floor itself. The player must be aware of the middle court line, however, if he has been moving in that direction. Although the move is spectacular it is relatively safe if practised correctly. As with the roll, it is important to teach players how far they can actually reach to retrieve a ball that is falling towards the floor in front of them.

(c)

b)

d)

(e)

Brazilian back-court player dives to recover Russian tip

Setting

Setting is the means by which the ball is put in the air close to and above the height of the net so that an attack player can smash it into the opponents' court. Although the mental and emotional characteristics of a setter are quite important only the physical side of the skill will be looked at here. First of all the player who is a setter should be a good volleyer and capable of putting the ball in a position for attack with accuracy and consistency. Although there is often a tendency to use the shortest players as setter this is not always the best policy. A team that can get six players on court who are all fairly tall will have an advantage, and there is no reason why a tall player cannot learn to set as well as a shorter player. The setter must be able to volley the ball from some difficult body positions when he is put under pressure, and must also have the ability to move to the position to set the ball. The

Luxembourg setter putting normal set to attacker number one in British Caledonian Cup at Crawley 1976

setter must be agile and fast on the court to perform well.

The first type of set normally used is the **high set** to either side line. The ball should go about 15–18 ft (4·5–5·5 m) high in the air and come down 1–2 ft (0·3–0·6 m) from the net about 2 ft (0.6 m) inside the antenna. Every player on the

team should be able to perform this skill and from almost any position on the court when need be. This skill is no different from the volley described earlier and the same technique should be used. The **short set** occurs when the ball is placed just 1 or 2 ft (0.3–0.6 m) above the net just

41

Brazil sets short against Egypt during Montreal Olympics

in front of the setter, so that the attack player must be in the air as the setter is passing him the ball. This play is used to confuse the blockers by either having the attack player hit the ball before the block is ready or holding the block in position long enough for the ball to be passed to another player who will have an easy hit around a poorly formed block. The setter uses little muscle in setting this ball since it does not have to go very far and he must time his set with the approach of the smasher. This particular play is spectacular and not as difficult to perform as it looks initially. It does depend, however, on a good first pass to the setter.

A **shoot set** is one that is passed on a flat trajectory

Korean setter (arrowed) moves very quickly into position after a strong Russian serve

quickly to one of the outside hitters. The object of this set is to get the ball to the attack player before the middle blocker can get in position to assist in making a two-man block. The attack player should be beginning his approach as the setter passes the ball to the position near the antenna for the attack player to smash. The set must be accurate because the attack player will not have time enough to adjust should the ball not be located at the correct place at the right time. The technique for the shoot set is somewhat different from the other sets. Contact with the ball at the initial stage of the pass is a little lower than with the ordinary volley. Also the direction of extension of the arms is outward rather than upward. The hands in fact should be pushed in the direction of the desired resultant set, i.e. 2 ft (0·6 m) above the net close to the antenna. It is critical that the setter judge the timing of the attacker's approach so that the player and the ball arrive at the point of

Luxembourg setter shoots the ball to the outside hitter against Scotland

attack at the same time. The amount of force applied to the ball will vary depending on how far the setter is from this point and how fast the attack player is approaching the net. The faster the set the more skilfully the two players must

work together.

The **overhead set** is used to set the ball to a player who is behind the setter. This can be either a normal high set or a short set. To achieve this set the ball is played almost on the top of the setter's head rather

orean setter calls for the ball while all players have turned to face the action

than at the forehead as in the forward set. The hands follow through behind the setter and he arches backwards as his legs extend to apply the necessary force to the ball. Using this technique the setter can keep his hands in contact with the ball just as long as he can in the forward set.

Note: It has been pointed out that for the different sets a somewhat different technique is used. Care should be taken to disguise as much as possible which set is coming by not getting into position too early with the hands, thus keeping the defenders guessing.

Movement

In the introduction to this chapter it was indicated that movement is probably one of the most important ingredients of successful volleyball. Probably the best way to approach this component of skill is to list the aspects of movement to illustrate the concept and its importance.
1. Before discussing the actual skills of movement players must understand where they should be located on court at any given time, and how to react to game situations even at an early stage. It is the job of the coach to determine the type of system that is being played for offence, defence and cover. From this the player should know where he should be on the court when any occasion arises, and he should be in the right place or trying to get there. Assuming this basic position on court as the phases of play go on should be drilled into the players so that they do not have to think about it and will be in their correct places automatically.
2. Players must learn to read the game from cues given by their opponents in the execution of skills, and from set patterns of play in certain situations. Many people have watched the 'old pros' in any sport who, though lacking in fitness or past their physical peak, still manage to cope quite well with their less experienced but more fit youthful competitors. They seem to be at the right place at the right time too often for the occurrence to be based upon luck. This is due to experience and the ability to predict what will happen from watching the performance of the opponents. The reaction time and movement time necessary to recover a hard-hit smash or a well-placed tactical ball will often not allow the player to carry the skill out in time if he is reacting to the release of the ball from the opponent's hand. He must be predicting what will happen from some earlier cue (line of approach, distance of ball from the net, hand position prior to contact, what the player had done in this situation before, or some combination of these). Although experience can be a great teacher in learning to read the game, training sessions can be structured to emphasise this aspect of learning.
3. Players must have the ability to cover ground quickly and this is largely a matter of

fitness and body type. The fitness aspects mostly concerned are strength, endurance and flexibility. Moving the body requires muscular strength, particularly when speed is required. Stamina is important to carry on doing the movements throughout a match. Flexibility is very important because of the positions sometimes required to play a difficult ball. If players are not flexible they will be using some of their strength to work against those of their own muscles which are unwilling to give.

4. Psychological factors are also important to movement, in that players must develop a willingness to move as well as a belief in how much ground they can cover to play a ball. This is partly the rationale behind some of the pressure drills used in teaching digging and diving. That is, players must get out of the habit of asking themselves each time 'Can I get this one?' before they move for the ball or decide not to go at all. That time used in asking may be the difference between playing the ball or not. Players must be encouraged to increase their range of effectiveness so that they can confidently cover their portion of the court under most circumstances.

5. The basic skills must be taught with some element of movement involved. There are some coaches who teach the skills in very simple drills that get progressively harder with little or no movement involved. Although this will result in good performance of the skills under the right circumstances, the player will have to learn to do the skill after having moved or while moving at some later stage in his development. Remember, good movement in volleyball does not mean simply learning to dive or roll and recover, it means being able to get into a position to volley when poor movement would have required a dig, or getting into a position to dig when bad movement would have necessitated an emergency play. It means being in the right place at the right time and being ready to move in the correct direction.

Offensive and Defensive Systems of Play

Because volleyball is a team sport with six players on court at one time it is important that they work together to achieve a common goal. To do so requires a system, or in fact two systems, with a third linking them: one with which to attack the opponents and one with which to defend against their attack. There is also a continuum along which the team moves in its transition from offence to defence and back again, but for the purposes of this text the two will be kept separate.

The individual player must know what his positional responsibilities are on court because he must work in concert with the other five members of his team. It is important that a player not only improves his skills and fitness but that he also has an awareness of systems of play and the manner in which his work is part of the team effort. A knowledgeable player will know the reasons for using different styles of offence and defence and be able to change from one to another without too much difficulty. Although it is the coach's responsibility to select the appropriate system of play it is definitely the player's responsibility to understand his assignments.

A team is on the offensive when:
- they are in the process of serving;
- the first pass of the ball is successful, i.e. the ball goes to the setter at the appropriate place;
- the opposition is in possession of the ball but are experiencing difficulty in returning it to the opponents' court in an offensive manner.

A team is on the defensive in the opposite circumstances:
- on receiving until the status of the service is determined;
- the opponents are mounting an attack from either a serve receive or a good first ball of any sort;
- when a team is having difficulty in returning the ball to their opponents in an attacking fashion.

The mentality associated with defending is different to that of attacking, and this must be kept in mind in the transition from one to the other. I call the transition stage 'flow' and it is important to note that often the change from offence to defence and vice versa is not instantaneous and must be looked upon as a tendency away from one towards the other. However, for most instances the rules of thumb listed earlier will serve to determine what positions the team should be in at a given time.

Prior to selecting a system of play for both offence and defence it is wise to set criteria for this choice.

Personnel

The type of system used should be based on the players that the coach has and not the players altered to fit into some system that is not suitable to them, though perhaps used successfully by some other team. It is too often the habit of coaches to use a complex system which another superior team finds effective even though the players involved in the coach's teams are not capable of handling it. As systems of offence and defence become more and more sophisticated (and this is the way they are ranked in this text) the demands on the players increase. It is also true that a team sticking to a relatively simple system when their skill level is limited will be more successful than if they use a system that is beyond their capabilities.

Look at the stature of your players to assess whether or not they can stand up to the requirements of the system. If the team is composed of short players they will not be particularly dominant on attack or blocking and you may have to look at some system that does not emphasise these points. If the team is big and slow-moving they may be weak in the back court so the

Russian women putting up a strong defence against a Korean attack. Player number four has the area outside the block covered

system will have to compensate. Normally a team is composed of a variety of body types and the best use will have to be made of the personnel available.

It is important to consider the experience of the individuals and the team in general before selecting a system. If the players are relatively inexperienced they will be working very hard mentally just to perform the fundamental skills. To clutter up their brains with complicated tactical

49

requirements will result in either a poor performance of the skills or the tactics or mediocrity on both.

The skill level of the players is important as well. In a relatively elementary system the requirement on the service receive is simply to get the ball in the air so that a second player in the front half of the court can set it to one of the attackers. As the systems evolve the requirements become much more specific and demanding on the skill of serve receive. If a team generally is mediocre in serve receive it should use a system that is not particularly demanding in that area.

Opponents

There is a tendency among some coaches to ignore what is going on on the other side of the net when determining the system to play and the tactics to put into use. Look at the team you are about to play with reference to the weak blockers, strong attack players, serve receive line-up, defensive systems, good and bad servers, etc. For example, if one of your opponents is a very weak server, than you are on the offensive as soon as he steps to the line to put the ball in play.

Accepted Systems

There is a fairly logical progression of systems for both offence and defence that is presented here and it is strongly suggested that in the early stages coaches make use of one of these. These are standard systems that are used by top teams and those developing as well. The essence of good volleyball is to make certain that a team is using a system that it can implement effectively.

Offensive Systems

This section will deal largely with the front-court players with a separate explanation on what the back-court players should be doing on attack cover at the conclusion.

Before getting into systems it is wise to reintroduce the reader to the numbering of positions on court as was shown on page 9. These numbers are position numbers and not shirt numbers, and the requirements for each position in each system refer to the player who is located in that position at a certain time.

Five different systems of offence are illustrated and explained here in order of difficulty. At what point a coach moves from one to the next or whether he creates a hybrid system off one of these is something he must determine for himself.

1. No Specialisation

In this system there are no special requirements placed on any of the players and each in turn becomes a setter or smasher according to the sequence of events on court. This system is purely a temporary one and almost an absence of a system of any sort; and for this reason should not be used for a long time in developing a team. It can be

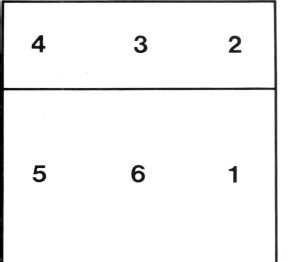

Court position
numbering system

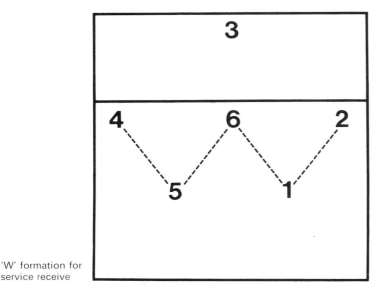

'W' formation for
service receive

used in early stages of development and in recreational volleyball and could probably be used by top-class players who are not accustomed to playing with each other but can work together in much the same way that jazz musicians can have a jam session.

In this system there is a line-up for service receive and position 3 is the designated target for first pass. The line-up for serve receive is called the 'W' formation for obvious reasons. In this system the objective is to get the ball to position 3, and whatever player is in that position at that time sets the ball to either of players in position 2 or 4. This is the case in both serve receive and defence. In this way all players get an opportunity to play in all positions, allowing the coach to assess the potential of his squad and determine the type of system towards which he should work.

2. Pairs System

In this system the players work in pairs as setter and attacker. That is, each setter sets primarily for only one attack player and the object of the play is to get the ball to the correct setter so he can mount an attack in conjunction with his attack player. There are certain advantages to this system. First of all it is moving towards specialisation of personnel as setters and attackers. Secondly, it allows each setter to become accustomed to one attack player, and the two can be encouraged to work out combinations of moves for certain situations. Primarily, though, they will be using normal sets at the position of the attacker. The diagrams opposite illustrate the front-court attacker and the setter who is working with him on serve receive.

There are some disadvantages to this system. First of all, since there is only one attacker designated in the front court in

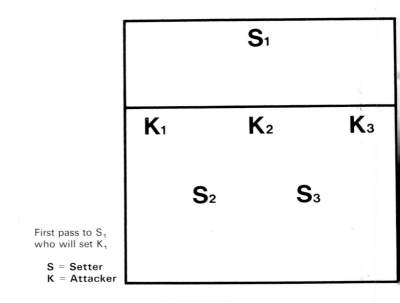

First pass to S_1 who will set K_1

S = **Setter**
K = **Attacker**

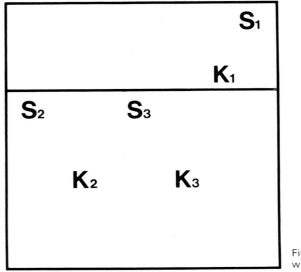

First pass to S_1 who will set K_1

each rotation, this makes the offensive system predictable, thus making the job of the defence easier. Secondly, half the time the first pass must go to position 2 and this can be a fairly demanding skill for beginning players. In some cases the wrong setter may be setting up the ball or the attack player will be setting to one of the setters or the other attack player. This defeats some of the advantages of the system. The demands of playing all three positions across the front court are great, and it is difficult for all players to learn the attack and defensive responsibilities and skills for all three positions. Again, this system is recommended as a transitory stage only, and should be used to develop a team and not as a terminal set of tactics.

3. 4–2 System

In this system the team is composed of four attack players and two setters. The two setters play opposite each other and when they are in the front court play in position 3 so that they can set to either side of the front court. This will require some simple switching and variations in serve receive line-up as illustrated. The rule on switching or changing position is relatively simple. When receiving service the players must be in the proper rotational order until the moment the server contacts the ball. As soon as the server touches the ball the setter may move into the centre of the front court and the attacker may move to the sideline. There are several advantages of this system over the ones listed earlier, and it should be noted that this type of offence can be used very successfully at a fairly high level of competition. Here we have again specialisation of hitters and setters. There are always two attack players in the front court providing an opportunity for a greater degree of variety in the offence and making it more difficult for the defence to assess. The demands on service receive are not great because

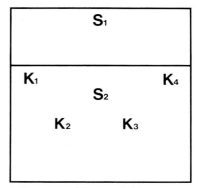

4–2 system with no switching required

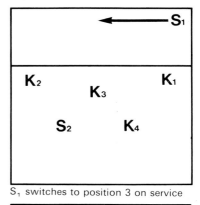

S_1 switches to position 3 on service

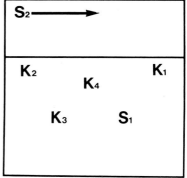

S_2 switches to position 3 to set to K_1 and K_2

Egyptian team receiving with a 'W' formation with number nine the setter

the ball need only be put into the air somewhere no farther than 10 ft (3 m) from the net and about 5 ft (1·5 m) from the middle of the court. The ideal target for the ball is the centre of the court and close to the net, but the system will still work even if the first pass is some distance off this. Either of the attack players may be set near the side line with normal sets, may come to the middle of the court for a short set, or attack anywhere in between the two positions. The setters and attackers can work out what sets they will attempt and when they will use them. The shoot set can also be used as well as overhead short sets. A variety of attacks can be implemented in this system, increasing the demands on the defenders.

There are some disadvantages to this system. Although there are two attack players in the front court at all times this still makes the offence somewhat predictable. The two opponents' blockers at positions 2 and 4 can key on one attacker at all times leaving only the middle blocker, number 3, in a temporary dilemma as to where he is going to have to block. This means that in most situations the opponents will be able to have a two-man block defending against the attack. In many teams the players doing the setting are not the tallest ones, and because of this have limitations on blocking. With this system the setters will have to be used on every block, thus weakening the system defensively.

With this system it is appropriate to discuss some basic offensive tactics.

(a) To optimise the attack, the ball must be set to the attack player who has the best chance of being successful. There is nothing wrong in giving the ball to one attack player if he is continuing to be successful and is not getting overtired. By the same token there is little benefit in setting a mediocre attack player over a weak block if he is going to be less successful than his team-mate on the other side of the court regardless of the standard of the opposition's block. It is the responsibility of the setter to determine where the best possibility lies and up to the coach, before the game or during times out, to assist him in doing so.

(b)   In most cases the diagonal shot is the easiest for the attack player to execute successfully since there is more room on that side of the court to hit the ball around a block. Line shots, though very good tactically, are difficult to execute and require a high degree of accuracy.

(c) Attack players must learn to hit the ball hard in match play situations and with control. Although off-speed hits and tactical balls are useful they are only successful because an attack player has established his ability to hit with power in the first instance. Players must learn not to hold up when under pressure.

(d) In some cases with a 4–2 system one of the attack players may come to the middle of the net for a short set. It is not always necessary to set to this player but he can be used to keep the middle blocker from moving away from the centre until it is too late to get a good block on the other attack player. For example, a player in position 4 may come in for a short set and the setter will pass the ball overhead to the player in position 2 for a normal attack. While this is happening the defending player in position 3 will have to remain in the middle of the court and may even have to jump with the attack player who is coming for the short set. For this reason it will be difficult or impossible for him to get to the outside position to assist on the block with his team-mate. It is on this fairly simple concept, 'holding the block', that much of the later offensive tactics are based.

(e) Since in this system players will be attacking in a variety of methods it is important to have the system co-ordinated. The person to call the plays is the setter in the front court and what he decides should be based upon the state of his attack players as well as the defensive line-up on the other side of the net.

The simplest method of making calls is by hand signals shown to the players before the ball comes over the net on service.

Some teams have the setter stand with his back to the opposition just prior to service, and he shows a certain number of fingers on each hand to the attack players to indicate what sort of set they should be getting ready for. If the serve receive is off target and the setter is having a difficult time to play the ball then the called play is off. The setter may cancel the play verbally as well.

4. 4–2 System with Setter at 2

In this system the team still has four attack players and two setters, but they now set up in a different manner offensively and specialise to a greater extent. The two designated setters will play in position 2 when in the front court and will do most of their setting from a position about 7 ft (2 m) in from the sideline. Two of the attack players will be placed in the middle of the court (position 3) when they are in the front court and they are the middle hitters and middle blockers. Although these players are needed for attack purposes and this section is on offensive systems, selection of personnel for this position should be based strongly on the player's ability to block. The other two attack players will normally play in position 4 when in the front court, and should be the best two attack players on the team.

When the setter is at position he will set from position 3 on service receive the same as in normal 4–2 system, but in all other cases he will set from position 2. The serve receive positions are shown on page 5 as well as the points of attack for the two front-court hitters.

There are several advantages of this system over the normal 4–2 system. First of all it is stronger defensively with the placement of a blocking specialist in the middle. The number of variations possible on offence is increased with the increased use of a middle attack player. This system allows for greater specialisation so that a player is always in the same position in the front court. In this way he will be able to reach a greater mastery of playing a certain position and not have his weaknesses taken advantage of as often as

The England team receiving a Danish serve with the setter at position two

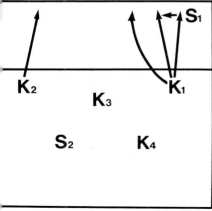

Setter at position 2. Three options for K₁

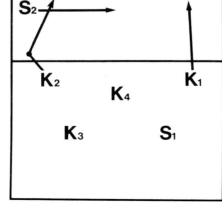

Setter at 4. Same as 4–2 system, setting from position 3

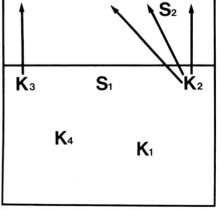

Setter at 3, sets from side. Three options for K₂

before. This is also a good system to use as a transitional stage between the 4–2 system and penetration by a back-court setter. It teaches certain concepts without the pressure of three attackers and the greater serve receive demands. It helps the setter to learn to set from one side of the court with two attackers coming in front of him and it teaches the middle player the techniques of hitting and blocking from the middle. It also allows the setters and attackers to work on some basic deception ploys.

There are some points to consider on the problems that may be encountered with this system. First of all the smashers will only be using two-thirds of the net through which to attack, in most cases. This can be compensated for by having the middle attacker smash from behind the setter (position 4) or having the setter smash occasionally, but a good defensive team would be prepared to shift their block towards the strong side the majority of the time. As the first

ball must be passed to the side of the court instead of the middle and also must be relatively close to the net if the team wants to use short attacks, the demands on serve receive have increased from the 4–2 system. If, after a fair period of trial, it is found that the ball is being passed in such a manner on serve receive that the setter is having difficulty in the majority of instances to set to the middle hitter, then the use of the system must be reviewed.

The team must have two players who can set and are developing into good setters. In the previous systems the demands on the setters were minimal and really any player on the team should have been able to carry out the necessary skills. In this system the setters will have to be making better use of the ball that is passed to them and this will be more demanding both mentally and physically. There will be greater demands on the players playing in position 4 for the attack as they will be expected to be

ready and able to hit on all occasions. The middle blocker will also be expected to take charge of the block, setting it in the right place and being the dominant force in it. The 4–2 system with the setters at 2 is an improvement on the ordinary 4–2 system; it is more interesting, has greater possibilities tactically, but is more demanding on all team members.

5. Penetration

Penetration is a system of offence in which a back-court player is used as a setter so that all the three front-court players are potential threats to the opposition. This increases the possibilities of attack immensely and makes the job of the defending team very difficult. But first of all, a word of caution. If a coach is interested in competing successfully and not just using a system for the sake of it he must be aware of the requirements of a team using penetration:

the team must have two good intelligent setters;

all six players on the team must be a threat on attack;

the serve receive must be good enough to get the ball to the position required (usually between positions 2 and 3 and about 2 ft (0·6 m) from the net) at least 75 per cent of the time.

To accomplish these objectives a coach must be working with players who have a lot of intensive training or a group who are working for a minimum of eight to ten hours per week as a unit. There is a tendency to use this system too early in the development of a team, and this results in unnecessary losses and corruption of the skills in an effort to fit into a pattern for which the players are not competent. There are a lot of interesting moves and variations that can be used in the other systems that can be as exciting as a poorly played system of penetration and also a lot more effective. Only a

short space will be taken here to describe penetration and only one system will be explained.

The setter will penetrate from the back court on only certain occasions:

on service receive;

on a free-ball situation;

occasionally when the first pass from the defence is good;

when the opponents' attack is blocked high into the air in the defenders' court and they have three more hits remaining.

The line-up for service receive on penetration is in the next column. Some coaches recommend that the setter should not penetrate from position 5 as he has so far to travel and on a poor receive will cause a lot of difficulties. In this case it is suggested that the other setter who will be in position 2 should do the setting and only two attackers be employed, the same as would occur in the 4–2 system with the setter at 2. During the course of normal play the setter

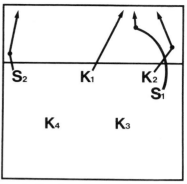

Penetration from 1 on service receive and lines of attack

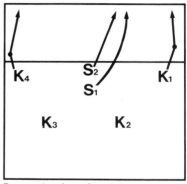

Penetration from 6 and three attack lines

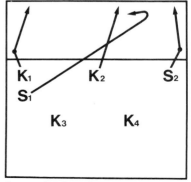

Penetration from 5. Note long distance to travel

The Danish national team using penetrating setter number twelve coming from position one

Following their service the English team players are switching into their specialist positions both front and back court

will switch in the back court to position 1 and will penetrate from there to the front-court position when play allows. In the case of the opposition being in trouble after their second hit and a 'free ball' being imminent the setter penetrates and makes this obvious to his team-mates by calling the play. The front-court players must then come off the net and player in position 6 must move to the right to cover the part of the back court vacated by the setter.

We now get to the objects of penetration in detail. The system is simply designed to confuse the blocking and the back-court defence as to who is going to hit the ball until a time when it is too late to make the necessary defensive adjustments. The simplest play is one involving the setter, player in position 3 and player in position 4. The opponents' blockers will be lined up on the three potential attackers (2, 3 and 4), and if possible will try to get a two-man block on whichever one is going to

Scottish men's team receives Luxembourg's serve and has setter (arrowed) penetrating from position number six

Defensive positioning with penetration system and first moves on 'free ball'
○ = blocker

Team positioning as ball crosses net and lines of attack

These two photographs show the essence of offence using a penetration system. The English setter between positions two and three has the option of setting any one of the three players in the front court. He has used players number seven and fourteen to hold two of the blockers in position and has then set the ball to the attacker at position four. The Danish team has only managed to put up a poor block

smash the ball. If the ball is set high in the air then the blockers will have time to decide to whom it has been set and develop a fairly strong block, perhaps even a three-man block if it is the player in the middle who will hit. However, if the player in position 3 comes in for a short set then the middle blocker must commit himself to that hitter until he is absolutely certain that he is not going to hit the ball. He may even have to jump with the attack player if the play is well executed, thus allowing the setter to pass the ball out to position 4 for the attack. Depending on the time it takes for the set to go to the attacker and the distance from the middle of the court it travels, the middle blocker will have varying degrees of difficulty in getting out to help his team-mate to put up a two man block. A hitter against a one-man block should hit around it on most occasions. This is only one simple play that can be used in penetration but it is the essence of the

game in this system. There are hundreds of variations that are possible, but the critical factor is the delusion of the block and back-court defence.
Combinations of short sets and shoot sets can be used but normally there is a safety valve in the play so that if the fast or difficult plays cannot be executed the setter can give a high normal set to his safety player, usually one at the sideline.

Offensive Cover

Although we all hope to have a successful attack when on offence, experience and statistics will teach us that often the smash is blocked and comes back into the attacking team's court. There must be provision made for this and an attempt to defend the court against a ball coming back off the block. This is offensive cover, or cover on the smash. Depending on the system of offence and defence being used it will be more or less easy to get players close to the attacker and a second line of

Korean ladies' team have all moved to cover their attacker facing a large Russian blocker

cover behind prepared to take up balls that bounce high off the block.
The more complex the offence the more preoccupied the non-smashing players will be, because of the deception tasks they have been assigned, but then if the tactics are working

the less likely the chance of the attack being blocked. It is important to have a system of offensive cover and even if every player does not get into the appropriate position on court he should be heading towards the point of attack, and anticipating the ball

coming off the block. There are basically two systems of cover to be considered: 1–3–2 where the first line of cover is composed of three players and is easily used in the less complicated systems; and 1–2–3 where the close cover is composed of two players backed up by three others some of whom were involved in the attack in some way.

Japanese attacker is covered by his two team-mates

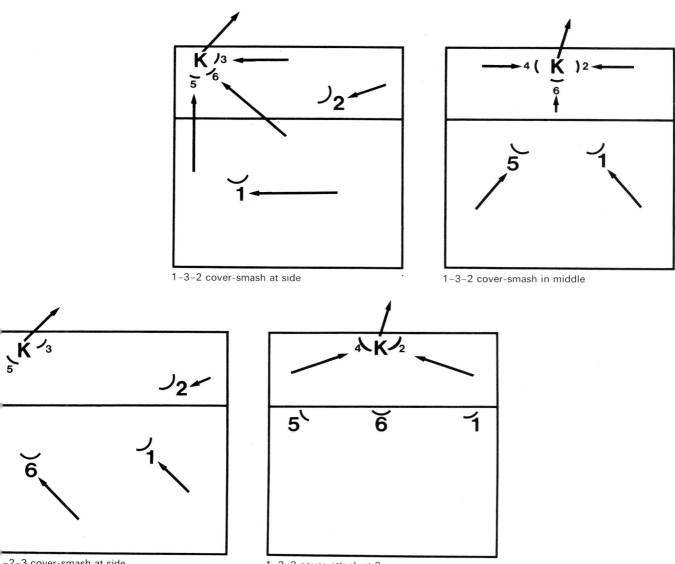

1–3–2 cover-smash at side

1–3–2 cover-smash in middle

–2–3 cover-smash at side

1–2–3 cover-attack at 3

The strong Czechoslovakian block provides a good first line of defence against Cuban attack

Korean ladies block Russian smasher down the line

Defence

It has been said that offence scores side outs and defence scores points; and as we all know, it is points that win the match. For the beginning player defence does not provide the appeal that offence does so that it will require considerable attention from the coach to assure that the team spends sufficient time on defence training. Good defensive play is founded upon good basic skills and the ability to read the opponent's play. Much hard and sometimes uninspiring work is needed to develop a sound defensive team.

Front Court

The first line of defence is the block and for this reason it is vital to have this area of defence strong. It is beneficial if the best blockers can play in position 3 as they will be involved in almost every block that is made. This should be a player who is tall and agile, relative to the standard of play. He must be able to get to the two outside positions to assist the other two blockers with their block as well as take charge of the middle block. Some teams use the outside blockers to decide where the block should be placed so that the middle blocker simply comes to them and jumps, forming a single block. Other teams may use the middle blocker to decide the block's location. It is important to make this clear to avoid confusion; that is, a team must use one system or the other.

Although the initial purpose of the block is to prevent the attack player from hitting into a portion of the court, it is wise to play the percentages. Against unfamiliar opposition or with relatively inexperienced blockers it is best to block the diagonal or cross-court smash. To do this, the outside blocker lines up so that his outside hand is opposite the ball at the point of contact. If a player is repeatedly hitting down the line then the block can readjust to block out this player. The outside blocker can move so that his inside hand will be opposite the ball, thus placing two hands in the way of the line shot. A good attack player will hit around the block when he is set well regardless, so it is important that the block effectively removes the possibility of his hitting to some portion of the court so that the back-court defence can line up accordingly. The basic positions for the front-court players on the block for the three main attacking points is illustrated on page 68. The shaded area of the court is the part that is protected from a hard smash.

The ball will not be hit into the shaded area unless:
- the block is poorly formed and the ball comes through;
- the ball is hit over the top in a looping shot and thus not a real smash;
- the ball is played tactically or tipped;
- the attacker can jump higher than the defenders and simply hits over the block.

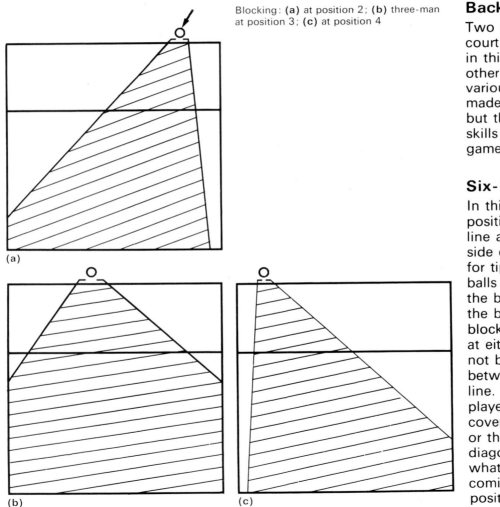

Blocking: **(a)** at position 2; **(b)** three-man at position 3; **(c)** at position 4

(a)

(b)

(c)

Back Court

Two systems only of back-court defence will be explained in this text. There are several other systems as well as various adaptations that are made off the standard systems but they all depend upon basic skills and ability to read the game.

Six-Up or Six Cover

In this system the player in position 6 plays on the attack line and moves from side to side during the play to cover for tips behind the block and balls that are smashed through the block landing just behind the blockers. The off-side blocker (i.e. front-court player at either position 2 or 4 who is not blocking) covers the area between the net and the attack line. The other back-court players at positions 1 and 5 cover for either the line smash or the remainder of the diagonal smash, depending on what position the attack is coming from. The basic positions are illustrated opposite.

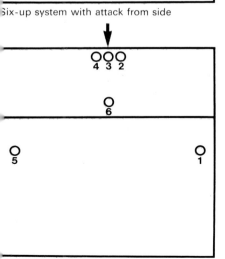

Six-up system with attack from side

Six-up system with attack from middle

Luxembourg team uses number six player for close cover behind block while Scotland attacks

This is a good system to use for beginning players as it clearly spells out the assignments and does not put too great demands on the players as far as covering ground is concerned. This is largely because number 6 is available to cover tactical balls and it is not necessary for the back-court players to come forward a great deal. It also makes it relatively easy to penetrate during play if the setter is placed at position 6 when in the back court rather than at position 1. The main weakness of this system is in the wide gaping hole left in the middle of the back court. An intelligent hitter can take advantage of this opening by either hitting looping smashes into that part of the court or playing a deep tactical ball in that direction over the head of number 6. On the other hand this is a good system to use when playing a team that uses a lot of tips and tactical balls.

The most common defence used in the Montreal Olympics was with all players back from the block

Six-Back System

In this system the player at position 6 plays within 3 ft (1 m) of the base line while the others line up in much the same fashion as in the six-up defence. Player number 6 has the responsibility for balls hit over or through the block into his part of the court and any high looping balls hit into the corners of the back court. The players in positions 1 and 5 as well as the front-court player not involved in the block have responsibilities for the smash into their court area but also for tipped balls in front of them. This system is more demanding on both the physical ability of the back-court players and their ability to predict what the attacker is going to do. This is because the defender must decide whether he remains back from the net to receive a hard smash or begins to move forward to retrieve a tactical ball. There is not a lot of time to make the decision. It is a stronger defence against a team that hits hard smashes most of the time. The basic positions and responsibilities are shown in the diagrams opposite.

England men's team uses number six-back defence in British Caledonian Cup against Denmark. The Danish attacker is aimed cross-court but has not cut his smash fine enough

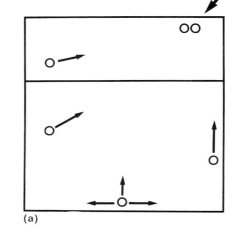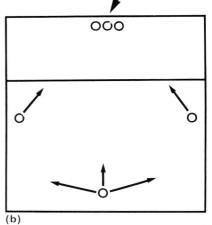

Six-back defences: (a) with attack from 4de; (b) with attack from 3. Arrows denote zones of responsibility

(a)   (b)

Drills

In this chapter some drills are described and illustrated for each of the skills and tactical situations included in the preceding chapters. The drills are graded into beginning drills to be used primarily for the initial stages of learning a skill; moderately difficult drills that can be used once players have some mastery of a skill; and pressure drills which are exactly that, drills that will put the players under stress while still demanding some performance of the skills.

There are a few individual drills included for improving each of the skills. Although volleyball is a team sport and in most cases it is best to train in a group it is possible to obtain marked improvement from individual training. The more times the ball is contacted in any of the skills the greater the player's development. Use of a wall to return the ball or drills where the ball goes into the air and returns to the player will all assist greatly in skill development. Individual drills can be performed outside or in

the confines of a relatively small room, thus adding valuable hours of training. Although it is the custom in many sports for the individual player to have his own equipment it is rather a novelty for a volleyball player to have his own volleyball as a personal property. Perhaps a change in this trend would bring about an overall improvement in skill.

It is important that the drills be done correctly and that the players are successful in their performance. If players are having difficulty with one drill there is little use in going on to something else before putting the present situation right. It is better to stop the drill, identify the problems and see if they can be rectified. There is no optimum length of time for a drill to last but there is a tendency for beginning coaches not to allow sufficient time for a drill to accomplish its purpose. Also, there is no need to introduce a whole slate of new drills at each training session as it is necessary for

the players to review time and again the basic skills, and time used to learn the moves in a new drill used to accomplish the same objective can be time wasted. When there are certain drills that a coach finds successful and tends to use repeatedly it is wise to give the drills a name, to save time in indicating to the players what is required.

As was written earlier, the drill here are graded in order of difficulty. There are an infinite number of drills that can be used in training for these skills and the coach is only limited by his imagination. In introducing the game and the skills, easier drills should be matched by easier versions of the game, whatever the age of the players. Most drills are designed to work on one or two aspects of a skill and this must be emphasised with the players. In the early stages the objective is to overlearn the basic skills, particularly the volley, dig, service and smash so that a firm basis for tactics can be laid down.

here are some drills here that re called pressure drills and re co-ordinated largely by the oach who 'feeds' the ball to e player(s) involved. lthough the coach can feed e balls to players at even the arly stage this is usually done y another team member with e players working in pairs or mall groups. The feed is a skill itself and the players must ppreciate the importance of eir learning the skill. A good oach must be an excellent eeder and all the players must e aware that when they are eeding the ball to a partner his arning experience is based pon how that ball is fed. In ressure drills the objective is stretch the player from rdinary performance to erformance under stress. The ress may be from having to ove farther to play the ball, om having to recover from laying one ball to having uickly to play another, or perating under extreme tigue. Caution must be used employing this type of drill nd pressure training is not

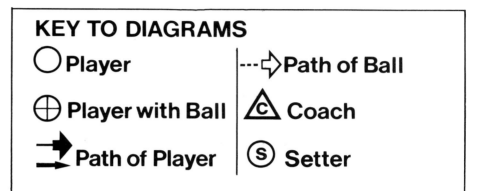

KEY TO DIAGRAMS

◯ **Player**

⊕ **Player with Ball**

➡ **Path of Player**

┄┄⇨ **Path of Ball**

△C **Coach**

Ⓢ **Setter**

appropriate in the early stages of learning a skill.

Drills for the Volley

1. Instructional Drills

(*a*)　*One player, one ball*. The player volleys the ball overhead to himself. The coach points out the hand position, the point of contact with the ball relative to the body and the full arm extension.

(*b*)　Same as the first drill but the player varies the height of the ball or moves it from side to side. The first alteration will assist in getting a better feel of the ball and the second part with the movement will assist

in learning to move into the correct position prior to playing the ball.

(*c*)　*Two players, one ball*. The first player tosses the ball just above his head and then volleys the ball towards his partner who is about 10 ft. (3 m) away. The partner moves to receive the ball and catches it just in front of his forehead and with his hands in the volley position. The coach should point out the necessity of moving quickly so that the ball can be received correctly, and the player passing the ball must learn that this will be more easily accomplished if the ball is passed high in the air.

2. Moderately Difficult Drills

(*d*) *Five to eight players, one ball*. This is called the 'shuttle drill' as the players shuttle back and forth after passing the ball. The players form two lines of equal size, with the first players of each line facing one another. The player in the front of one line has the ball and volleys it to the first person in the other line. After volleying the ball the player goes to the end of the other line; the player who is at the front of the second line volleys the ball back to the person who is now at the head of the first line. This drill can be made more difficult by (i) increasing the distance between the two lines, (ii) making the players pass the ball over the net or some obstacle higher than the net (the higher the better at early stages) or (iii) using jump volleys instead of normal passes. The coach must be making certain that the players are retaining good technique and that in particular they are not still running when they

Shuttle drill

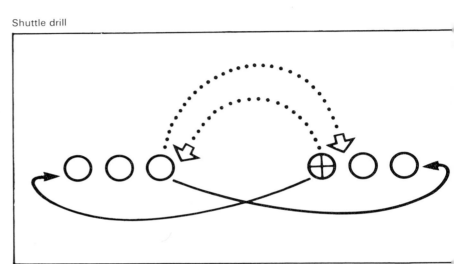

volley. Although it is possible to run and volley at the same time it is best to learn to move to the spot where the ball is coming and volley from a stationary position.

(*e*) *Shuttle triangle drill — four to six players, one ball*. In this drill the players form a triangle with the corners at least 10 ft (3 m) apart. There will be two players in at least one of the corners and it is here that the ball is first played. In this drill as in the previously described shuttle drill the players simply pass the ball to one of their

partners and follow the pass. However, instead of passing the ball back and forth it will be going around the triangle. I is an important concept that is being initiated here: that is, volleying the ball in a direction other than the one from which it is being received. The coach must make certain that the players have moved into position and are facing the direction in which the ball is to be passed. Care must be taker that the ball is not carried or double hit.

(*f*) *Two players, one ball*. In th

rill one player at a time is the eed player and the other player s doing the majority of the vork. The feed player volleys he ball in the air either to the ide of his partner, to the front r behind him. The second layer moves into position and asses the ball back to his artner. The first player then olleys it to some other spot, ausing the working player to

move to play the ball again. It will take some practice on the part of the players to feed correctly so that it is possible for the working partner to get the ball and still stretch him to a certain extent. The same points listed for the previous drill must be emphasised again.

Shuttle triangle drill

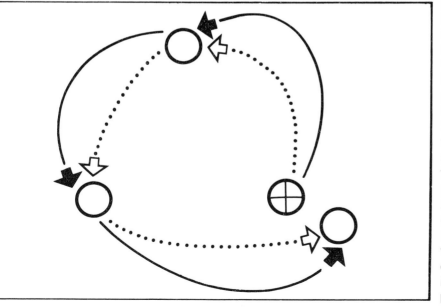

3. Advanced Drills

(g) *Three players, two balls. In* this drill two players are feeding and the third is working. The two feed players stand about 10 ft (3 m) apart facing the third player who is about 10 ft (3 m) in front of one of the feeders. The feed player he is facing volleys the ball to the working player who volleys the ball back. As soon as he completes the action of his pass he moves laterally to a position about 10 ft (3 m) in front of the other feeder. This player volleys the ball to the working player and it is returned in a similar manner. The working player moves back to face the first feeder, returns his pass and the drill continues in this manner with the working player shuttling back and forth. After twenty or thirty passes the players rotate their positions. Again the coach must make certain that the players are retaining the quality of their volleys. The main point in this drill is that the working player is in the correct position to pass the ball when it comes to

Advanced drill (g)

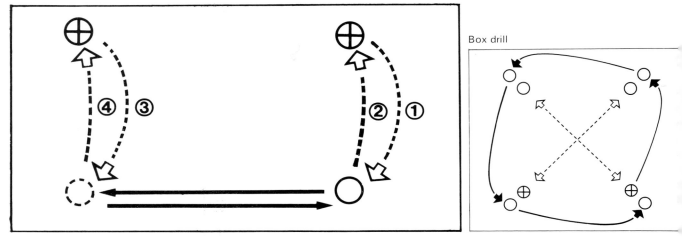

Box drill

him and is moving into position before the ball arrives rather than still moving when he is trying to volley.

(h) *Eight players, two balls*. This 'box drill' involves the players set up in a square with two players in each corner of the square. To begin with it is easier to do this drill with about 10 ft (3 m) between the corners but the distance can be increased as the players improve. The drill must be started with two players in each corner and the volleyballs in two corners that are not diagonally opposite. The two players with the volleyballs must start the drill

simultaneously. The interesting aspect of this drill is not so much the demands of the skill as the amount of other activity that is going on around the players during the drill. The balls will be passed diagonally across the square but the players will move around the square one position after each completed pass. The success of the drill depends upon a team effort and is a useful way of putting greater demands on players who may have become over-confident.

In many of the drills described it is possible for the coach to put a requirement on the number of volleys performed

without error, to give the players an objective measure of their skill level or improvement If in using any of these drills or others created by the coach, it may be wise to stop and discuss the problems (briefly) if they seem to be occurring throughout the whole group. It may be necessary to regress to a more elementary drill if the one being used is too demanding. Do not draw conclusions too hastily, however.

The dig drill in pairs

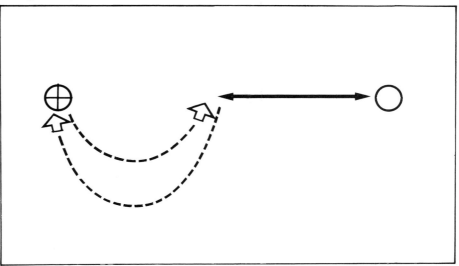

Drills for Digging

1. Instructional Drills

(a) *One player, one ball*. In this drill the player simply digs the ball to himself. Once he has some control he should be asked to vary the height, doing high and low digs alternately. The coach must be checking the hand position, the amount of arm swing as well as the point of contact with the ball on the arms.

(b) *Two players, one ball*. In this drill the two players face each other about 15 ft (4·5 m) apart and one of the players will feed the other for a dig. The player feeding should make certain that his partner has to move forward at least two steps to dig the ball each time. He is not to put the player under any great pressure but must instill in him the necessity to move to make contact with the ball. In this drill the coach must make certain that the points mentioned earlier are being adhered to but also that the player is assuming a low stance and is moving efficiently

to the spot where he will contact the ball. There is a tendency for beginning players to go forward with their hands clenched in front of them as they move and this takes away from their mobility.

(c) The same drill indicated above can be carried out with the feeder throwing the ball from above his head with one or two hands. Once the arm action for the smash is learned it may be possible for the feeder to hit the ball towards his partner, but a relatively high degree of control is necessary to do this. It is important that

the feeder temper the difficulty of the feed to the ability of the player he is feeding regardless of the level.

2. Moderately Difficult Drills

(d) *Three players, one ball*. In this drill the players are positioned in a triangle, preferably on court as indicated in the first diagram on page 78. The player with the ball at the start of the drill feeds to the player facing him who then digs it to the third player who is the same distance away as the feeder but off at an angle.

As in the volley it is important to learn to dig to a point to the side of the player as well as straight ahead. The feed should be in front of the working player but should not be more difficult than he can handle. Obviously as his ability improves the intensity of the drill will increase. The key point in performing this drill on the part of the digger is to have the foot opposite to the direction he wishes to play the ball in front of the other foot. That is, if he wishes to pass the ball to the right his left foot

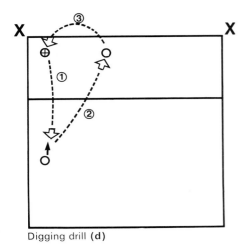

Digging drill **(d)**

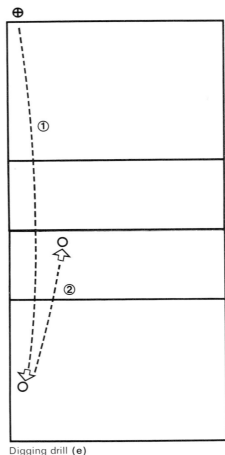

Digging drill **(e)**

should be forward and his body facing right. All other points of the basic skill must be retained as well.

(e) Three players, one or two balls. This drill is similar in design to the previous one except that the feed will be a serve and will come from the other side of the net. Because the drill is working mainly on the serve receive, it may be necessary to allow the feeding server to serve from closer to the net to assure his success on getting the ball to the receiver. The player receiving will pass the ball with a dig to the third player who is located to one side or the other of the digger and at the net.

(f) One player, one ball. To get in a lot of digging in a short period of time each player on a team can take a ball and dig to himself against a wall. If they are required to keep a specified distance from the wall (say 5 ft (1·5 m) and dig as many times as they can within a period of time this drill can become quite intense and be used as an evaluation device.

3. Advanced Drills

(g) Six to eight players, one ball each. In this drill the players stand in a circle and one player is placed in the middle. The player immediately in front of the middle player hits, throws or tosses the ball to him to dig back. As soon as he digs the first pass he turns either clockwise or anticlockwise to face the next player who feeds him for a dig as well. He continues turning around the circle facing each team-mate and may go around several times before he is replaced by one of the other players. The onus is on the players forming the circle to make the player in the middle work hard.

(h) Three players working, half a dozen collecting balls, about ten balls. In this drill the coach or a well-trained feeder will be hitting the ball to the three players involved directly in the drill. The coach will be located in the middle of the front court and the three players will be in the two back corners of the court with two in one corner. The balls are to be collected by the other players so that the coach will always have a ball with which to feed the working players. The coach will hit the first ball to a player in the corner where there are two players. After digging that ball the player will move to the opposite corner behind the player standing there. The coach will then turn and hit the next ball to the player in the second corner, who will in turn dig and then change corners. The coach will alternate hitting to the right corner and the left corner, and the players will move from one corner to the other after each successful or attempted dig. The players in this drill must learn to move in under the ball and practise judging where the ball is to be hit by observing the coach. He in turn must vary the intensity of the hits to the abilities of the players.

(i) One player working, coach feeding and the other players collecting the balls. In this drill the working player begins in the back court in one of the corners. The coach hits the ball

Circle dig

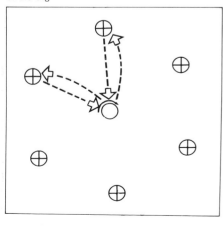

Back-court digging drill (h)

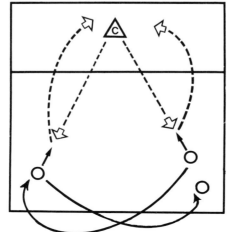

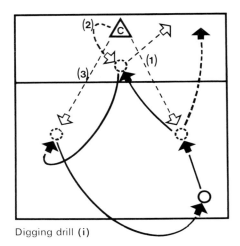

Digging drill (i)

Drills for the Serve

1. Instructional Drills

(a) Initially it is a good idea to instill the movement pattern of the underhand service in the players and this can be done most easily without having a net involved. Two players working with one ball could stand 10 ft (3 m) apart (at the beginning) and hit the ball back and forth to each other with an underhand motion. Each would catch the ball as it came to him and then hit it back in a serving action to his partner. Emphasise to the players that they should have **the feet firmly planted and keep the arm of the hand striking the ball straight** so that there are as few variables involved as possible. As skill improves the players should move farther and farther apart.

(b) Once the players have mastered the task of passing the ball a distance of 20 ft (6 m) with a serving action, they should be placed on opposite sides of the net to continue the activity. The same drill (a) is continued with each of the players moving gradually backward until they are able to serve successfully over the net from the serving zone at the baseline. This may take a matter of weeks and if you are playing some form of game in the meantime it is recommended that the players be allowed to serve from their own distance from the net for maximum success.

(c) Once players have developed the technique of serving over the net with a degree of success, the coach may leave them to serve back and forth to each other with half the team on each side of the net. It is better in many ways to serve from the serving zone but an idea of the serving success can still be obtained from serving from other positions behind the baseline.

to the player who digs it to the front court. The player then moves into the centre of the court near the attack line and is fed a ball to pass by means of a volley. The player then moves back towards the other corner of the back court but as soon as the coach tosses the ball in the air and raises his arm to hit it the player must stop and get ready to receive the ball in a dig. The critical factor in this drill is to teach the player moving into position not to move backwards when the ball is being hit in his direction.

2. Moderately Difficult Drills

(d) Once players can serve over the net it is a good exercise to put some pressure on them for placing the ball in the opponents' court with particular emphasis on difficult receive positions. Although there may be pecularities to your opponents' lineup or weak serve receivers to aim for, generally it is tactically sensible to put the ball in the back third of the court and particularly in the two back corners. With this in mind the court can be

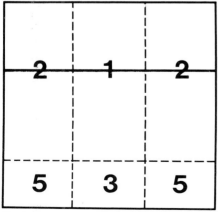

Serving zones

divided up into the indicated zones and contests held amongst the team members on the points achieved with a certain number of serves.
(e) Targets may be used on which to serve to encourage players to serve at specific zones of the court or on certain players. Chairs may be used for this purpose or towels may be placed on the floor to act as targets.

Note: Because serving is the first line of offence that a team can employ and because good serving can score easy points or at least quick ones, it is important at all levels of coaching that considerable time is spent on serving in training sessions. It is also important that any serving done in training be done with a purpose and with concentration, as practising a mediocre skill with a lackadaisical attitude will not result in improvement. Once a player learns to put the ball over the net consistently he must learn to serve to a target;

once he learns that he must learn to serve with force, and once he learns that he must learn to float the ball. Once he learns to do all three he must cut down on service errors. A team must learn to serve with authority in relation to its level of competition.

Drills for the Smash

The smash or the spike is a very difficult skill and as was indicated earlier has three basic parts in its makeup: (a) the approach, (b) the take off and (c) the smash itself. The first drills listed are used for instructional purposes.

Approach

(a) After watching the coach demonstrate the footwork necessary in approaching the net and getting into jump position the player walks through the procedure until he has the steps correct for the coach's satisfaction. No ball is used in this drill.
(b) After getting the footwork correct the player goes through

it with speed and does a quick jump at the end of his forward rock from heels to toes. The coach must make certain at this point that the player is not hesitating at the end of the approach and is getting some benefit in the way of transferred momentum and muscle elasticity.

(c) In the two first drills the player could be anywhere in the sports hall but now he is to test his skill against a net. This will check for the distance to be covered on approach as well as the forward motion on the jump itself. It must be emphasised at this time that the jump should be primarily up and down with little distance covered. The player must also learn to make minor adjustments in his approach so that as the pass from the setter varies he can approach slightly different points on the net with equal success. These adjustments could be made during either the first or second steps of a three-step approach. It is important to build in this flexibility at the early stages or a set pattern will become instilled into the player's approach which it will be difficult to change afterwards.

Wrist Action

Many players learn to smash a ball with no wrist action and though they may achieve success when they are well up in the air and close to the net, when this is not the case they will find difficulty in hitting the ball into court with force. Good wrist action puts top-spin on the ball and causes the ball to drop into the opponents' court, even when its initial path would seem to indicate it would be heading out of bounds.

(a) The player holds the ball in his non-hitting hand with his arm stretched out full in front of him. The hitting hand is placed beside the ball with the wrist kept loose. By moving the arm up and down quickly and keeping the wrist loose the hand will flip up and down in a relaxed fashion. After four or five oscillations the hand should be slapped down on top of the ball. This contact with the ball, though accomplished with a loose wrist must not be sloppy but firm as far as the hand itself is concerned. It may take some time to accomplish both of these at the same time but this simple drill will assist a great deal.

(b) Once the correct 'feel' is obtained in the first drill the player will now hit the ball out of his hand on to the floor. Still keep the holding arm at full stretch thus forcing the hitting arm to be fully extended on contact.

(c) Two players, one ball. The two players stand facing each other on opposite sides of the net and about 10–13 ft (3–4 m) from the centre line. The player with the ball tosses it in the air and hits it towards his partner with his arm at full stretch and wrist loose. The heel of the hand should make contact first and then be followed by the fingers. This should result in top-spin being put on the ball. As the players become successful at the beginning distance they should gradually move backwards until they are well into the back court.

Arm and Body Action

The most efficient manner to practise arm and the last phases of the body action in the smash is by hitting the ball at the floor. This may be done between two partners or with one player hitting the ball against the floor, the ball bouncing off the nearby wall and back to the player. Care must be taken to hit the ball with the hitting arm at the full stretch position. Also the skill learned in the wrist action drills must be retained or the player will be well advised to go back to that drill.

Approach Timing

The most critical factor in smashing is getting the body to the correct place at the correct time so that the ball is at the correct height and the player in a position to unleash his attacking arm at the right place, all at the same time. If the timing is bad the ball may still be hit but it will probably not be hit as hard and the attacker may not have the number of choices as to where he will be able to hit the ball were his timing correct. The main purpose of the approach and the jump is to get the player's body in the air as high as possible to serve as a platform off which his trunk, upper body and arm muscles can contract to smash the ball with maximum force.

(a)   In the first stages the player will not be hitting the ball but catching it at the peak of his jump with two hands, and with his arms at full stretch. The coach will toss the ball in the air to a position close to the net, similar to a set. The tosses should vary somewhat to test and encourage the adjustability of the smasher's approach.

(b) Once a player gets so that he can catch the ball in front of his hitting shoulder at the peak of his jump with some degree of regularity he should be allowed to hit the ball, if only lightly at first.

The remaining drills are simply different attacking drills that can be employed for warm up or for reinforcing the smashing skill. In analysing bad performance by a player it may be necessary to go back periodically to the various drills used in learning the skill in the first place, and this will be time well spent. Some players have learned to smash simply by playing the game and carrying out the whole skill at once in a game situation. These players may have the advantage tactically of being unorthodox but in many cases their performance is inconsistent and they cannot be flexible in some difficult situations. Also there is the added difficulty of unlearning habits that they have built up if they are to improve their skill.

Training Drills

(a) In this drill there is a setter at position 3, one queue of players with a ball each in the middle of the back court and another queue of players prepared to attack the ball at position 4. The players in the middle toss the ball to the setter who sets to the first player in the attacking queue. The player who tosses to the setter goes to the hitting queue and the attack player retrieves his ball and joins the queue at the back of the court. This drill could be run on both sides of the net at one time providing there are enough players and volleyballs.

(b) The same drill can be done with the ball being tossed rather than set. That is, the players with the volleyballs in the back court will not toss the ball to the setter but will come to position 3 and toss the ball in the air for the attacker to smash. This will be faster though not exactly the same as a game situation. This is an excellent way to warm up and

pick up the pace of a training session. The players will have to run between hitting and tossing to keep the drill going.

(c) Two setters on the same side of the net, two lines of attackers. Here the coach feeds the ball to the two setters in turn and they set to the respective corners. Once a player hits a ball he must retrieve one and place it near the coach or in an appropriate container.

Note: In smashing drills it is wise to have players other than the setters used to set the ball as this may happen from time to time in match situations. Also, when doing attack drills rather than having the setter in a static position have him move from some other location on the court just prior to setting. It would also be helpful to have the set come from various locations on the court so that the hitters can accustom themselves to the ball coming to them at different angles. This is all an attempt to provide realistic drills that are like match situations.

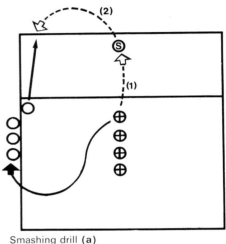

Smashing drill (**a**)

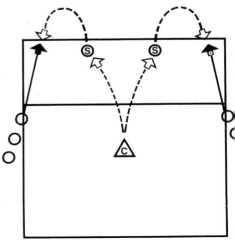

Smashing drill (**c**)

Drills for Blocking

In blocking it is important to get the correct jumping technique instilled in the players as well as the movement of the arms once the jump has been made. Once these have been learned it is necessary to teach movement along the net, placing of the block and the timing of the jump.

1. Instructional Drills

(a) Pairs jumping. In this drill the players are in pairs with one partner facing the other through the net. They jump together and touch hands over the top of the net without hitting it and without moving forward. This drill is designed to teach the jumping technique. It may be made trickier by having the players move one step to the side before jumping. This will make the jumping easier but will make the timing more difficult.

(b) Pairs with ball. In this drill the players are still facing each other in pairs through the net

but one player will have a ball and will simulate attack. The player with the ball will toss it in the air close to the net but only about 10–15 ft (3–4·5 m) above the floor and will do a short approach and soft attack. The blocker on the other side of the net must jump to block the simulated attack using the technique practised in the first drill. The coach may now point out the factors of timing, hand position and arm movement over the net and back. The attack player may be moved back from the net slightly to make the timing more difficult. The coach may now give some advice on the timing for the block: i.e. the further back from the net the attack, the later the jump.

(c) Blockers' movement drill. In this drill there are three pairs of blockers facing each other through the net. The coach is facing the net but one set of three blockers cannot see his signals. The coach will indicate by hand signals where he wants the block set, right, left or centre. When he signals the

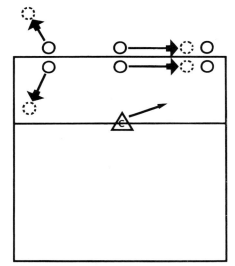

Blockers' movement drill

blockers facing him will move to the necessary position and will be followed by the three blockers who cannot see the coach's signals. The second group must react to the group who can see the coach. When the block is to the side the blockers form a two-man block only, and the other player not involved in the block drops back to the normal defence position.

In this drill the coach can check for movement speed and fitness of his players. It should be stressed that net touches are to be avoided. It was indicated earlier that the classic method of moving along the net is with shuffle side-steps and this can be emphasised as well. It is important that the players make an effort to move along the net in this way as it will cause the least interference with the net and other blockers, and will put them in the best position for the block jump. A coach may find, though, that in a match situation when a blocker has to move a large distance quickly, he will take one or two running steps facing forward and turn just before he jumps.

Once the blockers have learned the basic technique it is best to put them in a 'live' block situation where they are setting their blocks against hitters and are working in pairs or groups of three.

2. Moderately Difficult Drills

(d) Three blockers, two lines of attackers. In this drill three blockers are positioned on one side of the net and are faced by a setter and attackers prepared to hit from positions 2 and 4. The ball can be fed to the setter from a central source or from one of the lines of attackers. The ball will be fed to the setter who will pass the ball in random sequence to either position 4 or 2. In this

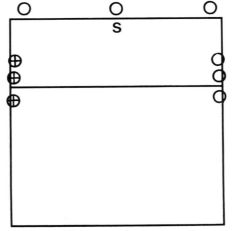

Blocking with two attackers

way the blockers will not be certain which attack player will be getting the ball thus simulating the match situation. As soon as the ball leaves the setter's hands the middle blocker and the blocker on the side of the attack, line up on the attack player and jump to block.

Using this drill the coach can make the following points:

- who is to set the block, i.e. middle blocker or outside;
- how to block the line and how to block the diagonal;
- getting the block together so that it is a unit and not a collection of arms with a lot of space between them;
- covering the angles so that players cannot wipe off a smash using the blocker's hands to advantage.

While this drill is going on it is best for the coach to stand in the end of the court near the baseline so that he can see what the blockers are doing in relation to the set and the attackers.

(e) Three-man attack. This drill

s the same as the previous one except that there will be three attackers against the three-man block. In this case it is much more critical that the blockers are able to 'read' what the setter is going to do with the ball. As was explained in the section on offence, the point in having a middle attacker is to confuse the middle blocker, and assist in getting one of the outside hitters attacking against a poorly formed two-man block or a one-man block.

Drills for the One-Hand Dig

At the risk of practising a bad habit, i.e. playing the ball with one hand or arm when two should be used, it is necessary for players to learn to control the ball when played with one hand as the skill is necessary under stressful circumstances. However, it would be unwise to spend a great deal of time on this skill at an early stage when players should be mastering the volley and dig.
(a) One player, one ball. In this drill the player simply keeps the ball in the air and off the ground by playing it back and forth from one hand or lower arm to the other. He should be able to play the ball high and low and gradually get complete control of the ball.

(b) Two players, one ball. In this drill one player is feeding the other to the side so that he will have to play the ball with one hand. The coach must point out that the hand held in a fist should be kept virtually perpendicular to the floor for the ball to be hit into the air and back in the direction of the partner.

(c) To practise this skill as well as flexibility and speed of movement players may get close together and play the ball between two or around in a small circle keeping the ball below chest height and off the floor.

Drills for the Roll

Once again caution must be exercised in spending time in doing drills on the roll when the team or club is at the early stages of development. The players must learn the fundamental skills of volleying and digging before spending any amount of time on the more sophisticated skills of the game.

(a) Initially it is best to practise rolling without using a ball at all. This may be carried out on mats at first but the sooner players can work on the bare floor the better. The coach must emphasise the rapid recovery to the upright position and the lack of injury in performing the roll. If the player is low and close to the ground to begin with he will not be likely to suffer any discomfort. Work on rolling to both the left and the right.

(b) Once the players can perform a roll, a ball should be placed on the floor to the side. The player can then take a step to the side, reach with the arm on that side, scoop the ball off the floor with the open hand and complete the roll. (Obviously the ball would not be played with a scooping

action in a match.) This drill is best done with a partner and rolls must be performed in both directions.

(c) The same drill can be performed now with the ball being rolled along the floor from the partner. This will add on the element of timing in the performance of the skill.

(d) Again the same drill, only with the ball being tossed by the partner and the ball being played properly with the inside of the arm or the closed fist.

(e) Several players and several balls. In this drill half of the players are in a queue at the back of the court and the other half are prepared to collect the balls for the coach. Each player in the queue moves to the side in one direction and the coach feeds the ball to that side for the player to retrieve and roll to recovery. Once the whole queue of players has gone through one way they repeat the drill rolling to the other side after retrieval of the ball. The coach is now in the position of feeding the ball at such a distance to 'stretch' the players,

forcing them to use the roll after their retrieve. He can also vary the toss according the different skill levels of the players.

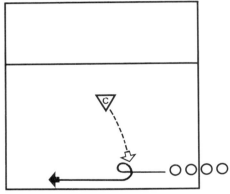
Roll drill

Drills for the Dive

The same factors regarding the time spent on training for the roll apply to the dive as well. It is a highly sophisticated and spectacular skill but is of little use if the players have not learned the basics properly.

(a) To begin with it is probably best to use mats. At first players must learn to accept their weight on their

hands in the form of a press-up. If a player is on his knees and falls forward on to a mat, catching himself with his hands and easing himself towards the floor, he will be able to predict if he is strong enough to do the same from a standing position.

(b) After he does several falls forward from a kneeling position he should do the same front fall from a standing position. It is not a bad idea to do a few press-ups before doing this drill to warm up the chest and arm muscles and thus avoid injury.

(c) The player is now ready to attempt a full dive using a mat first of all to land on for safety. He should assume a low position and then dive forward and accept his weight on his hands. Care must be taken to keep the feet and knees off the ground until the body has been eased back to the mat. That is, the hands hit first, followed by the chest, abdomen, thighs and then the knees will come to rest gently against the floor or mat.

d) In the next drill in the progression two players work together with one feeding the other. The feed is very important in this drill, as it must be difficult enough so that the working player must dive to retrieve it yet not so difficult that he will not be able to get it at all. It will take practice to achieve this happy compromise on the part of the feeder.

Drills for Movement

Although in most of the drills already listed for the various skills there is a reasonable amount of movement it is not harmful to do some activities that are dealing solely with movement itself. Not only are these types of drills useful, they provide a pleasant diversion from some of the skill training and are often enjoyed as such. The drills and practices that follow are only a sample and the coach should be able to make up his own once the first few are illustrated.

a) Shuttle run. In this drill the players line up on the baseline on one side of the court. They run to the attack line and then run backwards to the baseline; they then run to the net and backwards to the attack line. This goes on to the next attack line and then the baseline on the other side of the net. This drill can be done with the players moving with shuffle steps sideways. It can be made more interesting and demanding by making the players conclude each forward motion and backward motion with a roll.

(b) As players run in a warm-up they cross their feet over one in front of the other. This can be done when moving sideways as well.

(c) Players working in pairs chase each other. One player is 'it' as in a tag game and has a ball. Once he tags his partner with the ball he passes it to him and the other partner is 'it'.

(d) As players run they have to touch each foot with the opposite hand as the foot comes off the floor. They must alternate touching the foot in front and behind the support leg.

(e) All the players face the front and the coach states the direction in which they should move, alternating with forward, backward and sideways movement.

(f) The coach makes up a list of various movements, such as forward roll, backward roll, dive forward, side roll, front fall, etc., and reads the list off as the players go through the various movements. As the players improve they can do more movements in a time period or the time period can be increased.

Combination Drills

All the drills listed previously are primarily used for working on a single skill and this is a rather static way of training for match play. In the game players are required to volley, block, smash and dig and in no set pattern or order. So, for this reason it is a good idea to have drills that make match-like demands on players. Team members must have a certain level of ability to perform combination drills, because the opportunity to practise one skill depends upon the ability of the partner to perform the initiating skill. In these drills the variety is provided through one of two means: (a) The various players in a drill are all doing different skills and rotate around during the drill, or (b) some players are used to feed the working player(s) who is/are performing a variety of skills in sequence. Although these drills are more demanding they are also more interesting and more educational.

(a) Back-court drill for three. In this drill three players are involved using one ball. Two players stand with their backs to the net and the third (working) player is covering the back-court positions 1 or 5. The player towards the middle of the court is the target for the back-court player and is also the setter for the other player near the net. The player directly in front of the back-court player is the attacker. He will be alternately smashing the ball at the back-court player and tipping the ball in front of him. The object of the drill is for the back-court player to pass the ball to the player in the middle of the front court. When the ball comes to him he will set it to the outside player who will either tip or smash. In this way the back-court player will be digging a smash on one occasion and picking up a tipped ball on the other using a dive or some very quick movement into position.

(b) Once the team has a significant amount of talent to perform smashing adequately the drill described in (a) can be performed with live smashers. Again the player who is working is lined up in the back corner; the attackers, now on the opposite side of the net line up to attack from either position 2 or 4. Each attack player will alternate a hard smash down the line with a tip down the line in front of the attack line. The coach must make certain that the attacking players are providing reasonable tactical balls that

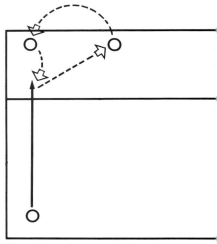

Tip and smash recovery drill

would in fact go over the top of a block and that they are attacking down the line and not in some other direction. The skill level of the attackers is very important in this drill.

(c) Recovery drill. In this drill two players are covering equally the front third of the court between the attack line and the net. The coach is on the other side of the net in the middle of the attack zone and is being kept supplied with balls by the players not involved in the drill. The coach tosses the balls over the net,

one at a time, sometimes alternating with the two players and sometimes not. The two players must keep the balls from hitting the floor by whatever means they can. They may be able to volley some of the tosses, but they may have to roll or dive for others. They must recover quickly. The intensity of the drill can be varied by the coach by altering the time spent on the drill, the rapidity of the feeding and the difficulty of each retrieve. It is important that the players go for every ball and learn to expand their range of effectiveness on court.

d) Smashing and digging drill. One of the most important and most difficult skills to learn is to read the smasher and the line of his attack. It is also difficult to overcome the fear of being hit with the ball unexpectedly on the face. This drill may help to educate players into reading the game better and in particular assessing what the attackers are going to do with the ball. The players are divided into

four groups and two players are used as setters. Two groups go to the back corners of the court and the players in each group will take turns in being the defenders of those zones, i.e. 1 and 5. The other two groups will become attackers and will be smashing from positions 2 and 4. The two setters will work with the two lines of hitters and face the line

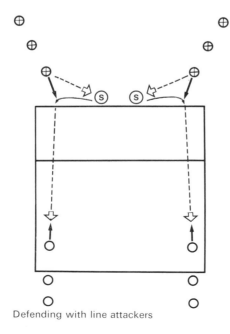

Defending with line attackers

for which they will be setting. The hitters will be instructed to hit either down the line (both groups) or diagonally. In this way the defenders will know which line they are defending against. It is important to put some pressure on the hitters to carry out their part of the drill correctly and perhaps some penalty for a missed smash could be applied. After a period of time the groups should change round so that everyone gets an opportunity to smash from 2 and 4 and that everyone gets to play defence in both corners with both types of smash. This drill can be very useful and should not be used unless a considerable amount of time (minimum 30 minutes) is available. Everyone should be required to set, as this type of setting is extremely simple and all players should be able to perform the skill adequately.

Fitness and Physical Preparation for Volleyball

Fitness is certainly one aspect of development in volleyball that the individual player can work on by himself. Fitness can be improved outside the actual training time and with sports hall time at a premium this is very important. By becoming stronger, more flexible, and having greater muscular endurance a player will add to his value as a team member, and if the whole team is more fit they may win matches that otherwise would be lost. The aspects of fitness that the athlete should be trying to develop are listed here and it should be a matter of personal pride that he improve in all these categories.

The times to become specifically concerned with fitness training are:

■ when club training time allows for fitness work during the training sessions;

■ when the group is sufficiently highly motivated to train independently from the club training sessions in pairs or small groups;

■ in the pre-season when

adequate training facilities for skill training are not available but the team members are available for training on fitness specifically.

Factors of Fitness for Volleyball

Although a general level of health and fitness is required to participate successfully in any sport, each activity requires its own specific type of physical development on the part of the players. Physical preparation for volleyball may be similar to that designed for basketball but will be much different to that required to produce a competitive weightlifter. The fitness factors important to volleyball are listed and explained here.

1. Muscular strength. Explosive muscular strength is necessary in volleyball for the players to jump high and to smash the ball with force. It is important for the players to develop speed of limb movement to accomplish these tasks.

2. Muscular endurance. Not only must a player be able to jump high and hit hard, he must be able to repeat this performance time and time again during a match or tournament.

3. Flexibility. Because all members of a team must rotate into the back court and play a largely defensive role during that phase of play, they must also be flexible so that they can assume a low stance comfortably and without unnecessary strain. It is also important to have flexibility in the joints so that in performing skills the muscles are not working against each other causing undue fatigue.

4. Agility. Players must be able to change direction quickly as emphasised in the movement section on page 89. This factor is related to both strength and flexibility.

5. Cardio-vascular fitness. This aspect of fitness is listed here last as it will probably be the last link in the chain that needs work. Because of the nature of the game of volleyball muscular

fatigue usually sets in before cardio-vascular fatigue, but the better this body system is working the quicker the muscles will be able to recover from local fatigue.

Principles of Training

1. Overload principle: In training in any method the body should be worked harder and harder as the sessions progress, if improvement is to be seen. Weights should be increased, repetitions added to, distances run made longer and the duration of drills lengthened. To manage this, a simple but accurate form of record must be kept so that the loadings can be increased from time to time and systematically. During the competitive season the overload and progression can be forgotten if it will interfere with the physical well-being of the player for matches. There is nothing to be gained from having the team members tired on match day from the week's training sessions. 'Don't leave your game on the training hall floor.' The greatest emphasis on overload and progression should be made in the pre-season training.

2. For strength training the load (i.e. weight or resistance) must be high and the number of repetitions performed low. For example in doing a bench press to improve strength, the weight should be set so that the athlete can press three sets of six to ten repetitions and the last repetition is the last he can perform with that weight.

3. To train for muscular endurance the load or resistance should be low and the repetitions high. In weight training this implies that the number of repetitions should range from twelve to over twenty using a lighter weight than in strength training. The same applies to methods of overloading other than weight training.

Weight Training

Weight training can be useful in building players up muscularly or retaining existing levels of fitness during the competitive season. Usually one exercise is done at a time with three sets of a certain number of repetitions. However, the exercises could be put together in a circuit with the athlete going from one exercise to another in turn. Generally, it is a good idea to do arm work last in a training session and not to work on the same area of the body with two exercises in succession. It is also necessary to exercise the muscles operating on both sides of a joint so that the athlete does not become muscle-bound and lose some range of movement. That is, if an exercise for pushing with the arms (bench press) is used then an exercise for pulling (curl) should be used as well.

England ladies' attacke[r]
smashes ball through a[nd]
space in the Finland
ladies' block during
Spring Cup in Denmar[k]

Exercises

1. Half squat or leg press:

This exercise is used to build up the muscles of the legs and buttocks used in jumping. There is a lot of a controversy about the wisdom of doing squats of any kind as there may be a tendency to cause injury to the ligaments supporting the knee joint. It seems, though, that half squats are much less dangerous than full squats, and since players jump from the half-squat position it would seem appropriate to use this exercise. Also, the tendency to cause injury from this type of exercise varies for individuals due to differences in their knee joints so that a period of experimentation could take place prior to putting this exercise permanently into a training programme. Because of the heavy weights used in this exercise safety is critical and it is best to use one of a variety of machines available for performing either the squat or leg press.

Leg press using a machine for safety

Half squat

2. Bench press: This is a standard exercise designed to improve the development of the pectoral and triceps muscles. Strength in these areas will assist in passing the ball with the volley over long distances. Again some caution should be exercised in this lift and a partner should be used to assist the working athlete if the exercise is performed on a bench.

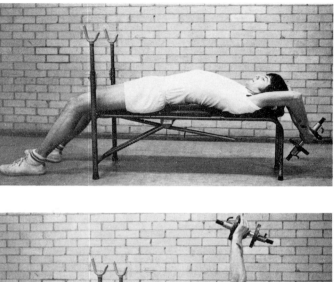

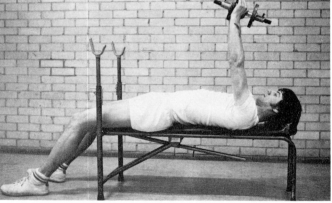

Bent arm pull-over using a dumb-bell for resistance

3. Calf Raises: This exercise can be done with the weight on the shoulders and the balls of the feet placed on a board two or three inches (50–75 mm) higher than the floor. This will provide for a full range of motion in doing the exercise. Again this work on the calf muscles will improve the player's jumping ability.

4. Pull-over: The bent arm pull-over can be performed with the athlete either lying on his back on a bench using a barbell, or dumb-bell standing up making use of weights connected to cables and running over pulleys. This exercise will assist in developing the arm and chest muscles used in performing the smash or service.

Sit-up on an inclined board using a weight for overload

5. Sit-ups: This exercise can be done with the aid of weights by using a small dumb-bell or just one of the weights itself held behind the head whilst performing the exercise. Additional resistance can be applied by having the player perform the exercise on an inclined bench. Since the abdominal muscles initiate the motion in the hitting part of the smash, this exercise will add to the ultimate power on attack.

Running

Running can be used as part of a general warm-up for training or for the development of strength and endurance in the legs. Since jumping ability is all-important in volleyball a lot of purposeful work can be done on fitness by designing a running programme specifically for the sport.

Because volleyball is an explosive sport, running training should concentrate on sprinting and resistance work. Short bursts of speed running can be interspersed with jogging or walking in much the same way that sprinters train. It is also useful to run up hills or with some other resistance such as running sand dunes or with a rubber tyre being dragged behind. Although a good volleyball player should be able to run a mile in a respectable time, running training for this sport should consist primarily of short distances with a high intensity of work load.

Bounding

There is now a tendency in the athletics world to use methods of overloading training other than weight training. That is, the athletes make use of their own body weight instead of some artificial method of applying a load. There are certain advantages to this type of training: (a) the movements are carried out at a speed similar to that used in competition, (b) there appears to be less tendency of injury in the transition from fitness training to competition, and (c) the demands on equipment are less than with weight training.

The basic idea in bounding is that through a series of exercises the player is asked to use his muscles explosively against the body weight only. The simplest form of this type of activity would be to get a player to jump as high as he can or as far as he can in a single or series of jumps. However, it is more interesting and easier to measure and motivate if certain gimmicks

can be used to implement this form of training. Some of the types of bounding activities are listed here.

1. Elastic rope jump: In this exercise a length of elastic is stretched between two secure uprights and a player jumps back and forth over the rope. The type of jump is not so important but it would be useful if it simulated a match skill and that the type of jump remain the same from session to session so that progress can be measured. The intensity of the jumping can be varied in the same manner as with weight training, i.e. low height of rope and lots of repetition or high rope and only a few efforts. An elastic rope is used to avoid injury if the jump is missed. (*Note*: an elastic rope is not an unusual piece of equipment but simply the elastic used by dressmakers that can be purchased in many shops.)

These photographs illustrate the nature and use of the elastic rope. A variety of other exercises can be devised, but in each case there is no danger of injury

improving the jumping ability of the players may be used, only two or three measuring devices should be involved in an effort to keep the data collection as simple as possible.

Flexibility Exercises

The importance of flexibility has been explained earlier in this section, and the exercises used are best shown by photography rather than verbal description. It is important to note that the idea of fast jerky motions in doing flexibility exercises has gone somewhat out of fashion and in these exercises the stretch of the muscle, whether it is self-imposed or done by a partner, is carried out in a slow, gradual manner. A good rule of thumb is to put the muscle under stretch for a count of five and then relax for a count of five and put it under stretch again. When a partner is doing the pushing it is up to the person who is being stretched to make a conscious effort to relax his muscles and 'go with' the push.

2. Standing long jump:
Using a starting line marked out on the floor with marking tape and having a tape measure attached to the floor, members of a team can measure their comparative jumping distances on a single, double or triple long jump. Competition and measurement make the exercise interesting and motivating.

3. Combinations: Any combination of jumps, hops and steps can be made up to challenge and improve the athlete; the coach is limited only by his imagination. As with weight training it is essential to keep some form of record on the achievements and improvements of the team members. For this reason, though several techniques of

A variety of flexibility exercises in pairs

Training and Practice Plans

The type of training a coach does with his team will depend upon certain factors.

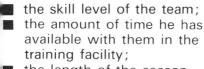

- the skill level of the team;
- the amount of time he has available with them in the training facility;
- the length of the season and the length of time he has contact with them throughout the year.

Ideally the coach would have contact with his players twelve months of the year for about twelve hours or more per week. However, this is not the case as many clubs have only one or two short training sessions during a relatively short season. Nevertheless, the format of the training season and the training sessions should remain about the same. Only the time allocation will be different.

The training session itself can be divided into separate sections for the purposes of organisation. The system used by the author is listed here.

Dividing the Session

1. Chat Session

Because a certain amount of talk has to go on within a club or team it is best to schedule a specific time for this and the best time is just prior to the active part of the training session. Time spent talking should not be during the training session itself because it holds up the training and also wastes the valuable sports hall time. The talk session should include:

(a) What is going to take place during that particular session in the way of new drills or tactics. This will save time in setting up the new drills as they can be explained on a blackboard beforehand.
(b) Any club administration should be done during this session rather than after the training session because many people wish to depart immediately.
(c) It is also a good time for some feedback from the players on proposed training procedures, previous sessions and perhaps previous matches.
(d) Assignments for administration and equipment can be set at this time avoiding any confusion later.
(e) Team tactics and their rationale can be discussed in relative comfort rather than during the training session itself. Again this makes more economical use of the sports hall time.

2. Warm-Up

It is important that the players have a good and thorough warm-up prior to beginning the training session proper, and it is equally important that the training session should not drag so that players have the opportunity to get cold during the session. The warm-up can consist of a combination of general exercises and volleyball skills. If skills are used care should be taken to make the drills fairly easy, allowing the players gradually to work themselves into the session. A certain amount of time should be spent stretching to avoid strain or injury later.

3. Grooving on Skills

In this part of the session the players will be involved in carrying out drills with which they are familiar, reinforcing skill patterns that they have already learned. The coach must insist that these drills be carried out to perfection and the level of drill will become more difficult as the players improve. A considerable amount of time must be spent on this type of activity to assure that the players do not lose what they have learned. The more times the ball is volleyed, dug and smashed the more ingrained the skill is in the player and the more dependable he will be in a match situation.

4. Something New

Every session must have something new and it should be introduced when the players are still relatively fresh, both mentally and physically. The coach should already have explained what he is to introduce during the pre-training talk session so that a limited amount of discussion should take place during the activity itself. The new material could be skill, tactics, a play to be used in certain situations, a drill of higher intensity, type of conditioning activity. This does not have to be anything drastically different and it could be the same for several sessions in succession.

5. Team-Type Drills

By this point in the session the players should be showing some signs of fatigue similar to the game situation. It is at this time that the team-type drills should be practised so that the players have not only to carry out the skills, but think about them as well as work under the pressure of tiredness. Although the skills should be carried out in a correct manner the importance of this aspect of the training session is to get the players into correct habits as regards positions on court, responsibilities at each phase of the play and timing for moves. If everyone is at the correct place at the correct time but the drill breaks down because the skill is not performed correctly, that is a separate problem and must be worked on at a different section of the training session. It may be necessary to go through team-type drills in slow motion or half-speed. The important objective at this time is the location of the players and their timing in getting into position.

6. Conditioning

Although a certain amount of fitness work has been done in the course of the training session through the drills, the emphasis has been on good performance rather than pressure. Conditioning drills can be made up of exercises (jumping, running, circuit training) or pressure drills where the game skills are practised under pressure situations. Whatever is used the players must be taxed physically with particular emphasis on jumping, flexibility and upper body strength. Work on muscular endurance is more important than cardio-vascular endurance, so exercises should be of short but intensive duration.

7. Feedback

Do not waste time in the training session itself for discussion on procedure unless absolutely necessary. Reserve some time or at least the opportunity for some feedback from members of the team at the end of the session. There is a lot of room for debate and opinion in coaching volleyball and the more discussion the better. It is much more effective to have team members believing in what they are doing on court rather than carrying it out because they have to. The coach can always stand to learn something from the players in any case. Some sample coaching sessions are given on pages 109–11 for your consideration.

The following are some points or tips that may be useful to the beginning coach.

1. Most of a training session should be involved with familiar drills. By giving each of the standard drills a name it will make it easy for players to begin without any undue amount of hesitation and instruction.

2. Drills should always be used for a long enough period of time. There is a great tendency on the part of some coaches to do as many drills as they can in a training session, never allowing the players to 'get into' any one of them. If the coach is uncertain when to change a drill, chat with the players for their feelings.

3. When instituting a new drill or a new skill resist the temptation to stop and correct too early on. Let the drill go on for five minutes to provide the players the opportunity to settle into it. If there is utter chaos and the behaviour is totally wrong do not hesitate to stop the drill immediately.

4. In establishing a drill make certain that it is being performed correctly and that the players are working on the right aspect of a skill or tactic.

5. Drills must get more difficult as the skill level of the players develops.

6. Poor technique must be corrected at all stages and a return to basics must be made if necessary.

7. It is not possible to teach skill very quickly and 'over-learning' comes only with great repetitions. Getting rid of a bad habit and replacing it with the correct movement is even more difficult and time must be allowed for this to take place.

8. As often as possible drills should relate to match situations.

9. At some time in the training session players should have to perform the skills under conditions of fatigue so as to simulate match conditions.

10. It is useful sometimes to set concrete objectives in drilling on skills. For example two players could be told to volley the ball back and forth between each other thirty times in succession from a distance

of 25 ft (7·5 m) apart.

11. Assign penalties for poor performance, i.e. press-ups, sergeant jumps, etc.

12. Do not get unduly concerned over temporary lethargy on the part of players during training unless it becomes a permanent situation.

13. Some form of novelty should be added to training from time to time. For example have music playing during the session, or set up an obstacle course for conditioning.

14. Emphasise service and service receive.

Parts of the Season

Once again this section may not apply to a number of teams that play volleyball for only a short period of time during the year, but for clubs that are involved in the game for a long season it is wise to look upon it in four sections.

1. Pre-Season

This is the time of year when the team is just getting back together and starting to make plans for the coming season's play. At this time of the year the players should be working a great deal on their physical preparation and a fair bit on regrooving the skills and the development of new skills. Tactics, with the exception of the very basics, can be ignored at this time. Players should be getting into a fit state and back into the habit of performing the game skills.

2. Early Season

This is the time of year when a few matches are being played but not the most important ones. There is time here to try out tactics and see how players are performing. It is important to arrange the team's tactics around the personnel available and not to force a system on the players just because it has been used successfully by another coach. Work should continue with the skills and enough conditioning should be done to improve the players physically.

3. Peak Season

During the competitive season the majority of work is done on skills and tactics. It is during this time that training sessions will be spent in preparing for the next opponent tactically and specifically. The tactics will have to be governed according to the personnel and their skill level at that time but some thought should go into preparing for each match tactically. Enough work should be done on conditioning to retain the present level of fitness.

Off Season

Some people would say that there is no off season, just a period of time between the end of one season and the beginning of the next. The attitude taken towards this period of time will vary according to the intensity of the competitive season and its effect on the players. In any case the players should not use the time to relax entirely, getting flabby and out of condition; it will make getting started for the next season even more difficult. The following are some ideas with which to fill this time period.

(a) A complete departure and rest from volleyball is the practice of some players. They become involved in some other sport that keeps them fit but participate in a relatively non-serious manner and get a mental rest from the season past.

(b) In the case of developing younger players in volleyball the off season is an excellent time for intensive skill training courses where improvement can be accelerated through day-long sessions over a period of several days. Working under other coaches and meeting other players can give added stimulus to the players.

(c) Non-serious play is used in some degree of success. Again, of 'keeping the hand in' on skills. Tournaments for three-man teams, beach volleyball, mixed volleyball and other such events have been used with

Year's plan

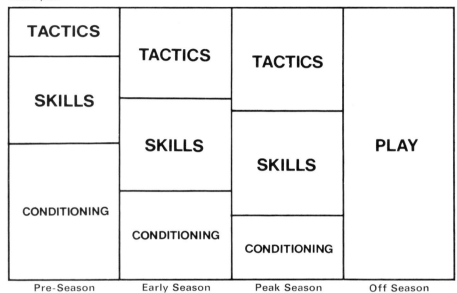

TACTICS	TACTICS	TACTICS	
SKILLS	SKILLS	SKILLS	PLAY
CONDITIONING	CONDITIONING	CONDITIONING	
Pre-Season	Early Season	Peak Season	Off Season

some degree of success. Again playing in this way helps to retain some fitness level while not taxing the players mentally and emotionally.

The diagram above illustrates the manner in which the year's plan should be broken down.

Top ladies' team in the world, the Japanese women

Practice Plans

Early Season

1. Warm-Up

- run 4 laps of court
- run 4 laps of court sprinting the lengths
- run 4 laps of the court doing crossover steps facing outwards one lap and facing inwards the next.
- run 4 laps of the court doing one length with a series of two-footed long jumps and jogging the rest.
- stretching in pairs: forward press, trunk twist, shoulders stretch
- 20 seconds' press-ups
- 20 seconds' sit-ups
- repeat

2. Skills Grooving

(a) *Volleying:* (i) in pairs 20 ft. (6 m) apart. ×50.
(ii) in pairs with one partner moving the other around to retrieve the ball with a volley. ×30.
(iii) in 4s in a triangle. Volley to a partner and follow the pass. ×100.

(b) *Digging:* (i) in 3s and in a triangle. One player feeds, one player digs, and the other retrieves. ×30 each.
(ii) same drill only with the feed being more difficult.

(c) *Smashing:* There will be two queues of players on each side of the court and one setter at position 3 on each side as well. The queue of players in the middle of the court will feed the ball to the setter who will set to the queue at the sideline. The attacker will collect a ball and join the feeding line. Attacking will be from 2 and 4.

(d) *Serving:* 50 serves each with half the team on each side of the net.

3. Something New

This will depend upon the level of the team.

4. Tactics

Defence practice. Six players line up on court in defensive positioning. The other players are on the other side of the net forming queues of attackers at positions 2, 3 and 4. There will be a player setting at 3. The feed will come from one of the lines of attackers and the setter will pass the ball so that it can be attacked from one of the three positions. The defence will have to react accordingly. The number of lines of attackers will vary with the level of competition and the type of opposition the team is likely to be facing. The players should change positions about every five minutes or the whole group can rotate one position more often. It would be worthwhile to spend a minimum of half an hour on this drill.

5. Conditioning

Circuit training will be used with the players going through the eight stations as quickly as possible three times. The coach should keep a record of the finishing times.
(a) 10 press-ups
(b) 10 sit-ups
(c) 10 sergeant-jumps
(d) Maximum number of pull-ups

(e) Shuttle run 3×33 ft (10 m)
(f) Jump on and off 20 in. (500 mm) bench ×20
(g) 25 wall volleys
(h) 10 V-sits (sit-ups).

Peak Season

1. Warm-Up

- run 10 laps of court
- stretching exercises 5 minutes
- run sidelines and use shuffle steps to run across the net doing at least three blocking jumps each trip across
- 1 v. 1 volleyball. This can be played with one player against one allowing three hits on either side or with a third player acting as setter for both players and passing under the net after each completed attack. Make use of the lines on the floor from other sports for boundary lines.

2. Grooving on Skills

(a) digging. The coach feeds the ball to the three players alternating corners in the back court. The players not involved in the drill collect the balls and then rotate into the drill in turn. Minimum of 50 digs for each player.

(b) Smashing. The players form two queues on one side of the net. One queue is in the middle of the court and each player has a ball. The other queue is lined up and prepared to hit from either position 2 or 4 . The player with the ball feeds it into the air as in a set and the player in the hitting line comes in and smashes the ball. Once he hits he collects a ball and once he feeds he joins the attacking line. The pace of this drill should be fast.

(c) Volleying. Work in 3s with two players feeding a third who shuttles back and forth between the two of them. × 30.

(d) Serving. In 3s. One player serves, second player receives with a dig and third player retrieves the dig. 15 serves and then rotate.

3. Something New

Again this will depend upon the level of the team.

4. Tactical Work

The next opponents tend to tip a lot on attack so a similar drill to that used in the practice plan A will be used but the attacking players will be asked to tip the ball into the weak areas of the defence a high proportion of the time. The coach will have to establish whose responsibility various areas of the court are for this type of attack.

5. Conditioning.

A repeat smash drill will be used. In this drill the player who is working lines up on the attack line and smashes a tossed ball and returns to the attack line ready for the next ball to be tossed in the air and smashed. The other players collect the balls and line up to pass them to the coach who is feeding the attack player. Everyone goes through the drill several times with the number of smashes required being reduced on each trip (i.e. 10, 8, 6, 4). Only successful smashes may be counted and the ball should be tossed high enough in the air to allow for the smasher to use a full approach.

Off Season

1. Warm-up

Five-a-side football.

2. Grooving on Skills

a) Volleying in pairs. After each volley the player who has just completed his pass sits down and then stands up in preparation for the next volley. ×20.

b) Digging in 3s, keep the ball off the floor as long as possible.

c) Smashing in 4s. Player on far side of net tosses the ball to a player in the back court opposite. This player digs the ball to a setter close to the net who sets to the hitter. After about 15 times, players rotate their positions.

d) Serving. Line up at each end and take 50 serves.

3. Triples Tournament

Line all the players up in order of height and divide the total number by three (hopefully it will work out evenly.) Number the players off by this number (if there are 18 there will be 6 teams) until you get to the end of the series and then number off backwards with the players and then forwards again when you reach the end of this second series. The players with the same numbers are on the same teams. In this way if you have a line up of 18 players the numbers will run as follows: 1, 2, 3, 4, 5, 6, 6, 5, 4, 3, 2, 1, 1, 2, 3, 4, 5, 6 in the order of their height. The type of competition played will depend on the court space and the time allotted.

4. Conditioning

All the volleyballs are brought out and placed on the floor. The players are divided into two groups, one at each end of the court. For a time period of one minute the objective of each team will be to keep as few volleyballs in their end of the court as possible. They may roll, smash, volley, throw or toss the balls to the other end of the court but may not kick them. They may not enter the other half of the court. This may be played for best of 5 and will stimulate a lot of activity if entered into in the right spirit.

Capacity crowd for the ladies' Olympic final at the Montreal Forum. Japanese attacker, Takato Shirai, hits over Russian block

Glossary of Volleyball Terms

Attack line: The line on each side of the net that runs from one side of the court to the other and is three metres from the centre line. Players in the back court may not attack from in front of this line.

Back-line player: Player who is in the back court at the moment of service occupying position 1, 6 or 5.

Block: This is the play made at the net by one, two or three of the defending players in an attempt to prevent the attacker from smashing the ball into their court.

Dig: The two-hand underhand pass where the ball is played on the forearms.

Dive: An emergency defensive play where the player must dive forward to retrieve a ball and absorb the force of his body falling toward the floor with his arms.

Feed: The technique of passing or tossing a ball for a partner to play in drill situations.

First pass: The initial pass of the ball either on serve receive or defence. More often refers to serve receive.

Match: In volleyball normally best of five sets with the team who wins three sets first being the victor. In occasional circumstances matches can be played best of three.

Penetrating setter: A back-court player who is used as the setter when a team is on attack allowing for the possibility of three attack players.

Roll: A means of avoiding injury when a player has to reach a long way to the side to play a ball with one hand.

Serve: The act of putting the ball in play at the beginning of each rally.

Set: A set is won when one team has scored fifteen points and is ahead by two clear points.

Setter: The player who puts the ball in the air close to the net for an attacker to smash into the opponents'

court. The set is usually the second pass and is normally carried out with a volley.

Shoot set: This is a set that travels very quickly from the setter to the attack player and will follow a line almost parallel to the floor.

Short set: This is a set that does not go very high above the net and is close to the setter when the attack player smashes it. (Also called quick attack.)

Smash, spike, attack: The act of hitting the ball downward into the opponents' court with force.

Substitution: The act of replacing one player on court with one of the substitutes on the bench. There are six substitutions possible per set.

Switch: This occurs when players in either the front court or the back court change positions with each other. This may be done only after the server has contacted the ball.

Tip, tactical ball or dump: In this play the attack player,

Bibliography

rather than hitting with force, will pass the ball just over the block or deep to the back court. This can be done with one or two hands, but is normally done with the finger tips of the attack hand.

Volley: The two-handed overhand pass where the ball is played on the fingertips of the two hands.

American Association of Health, Physical Education and Recreation, *Skills Test Manual: Volleyball* (1969).

Anthony, D. A., *Volleyball, Do It This Way* (Faber and Faber).

Anthony, D. A., *Success in Volleyball*.

Bratton, R. D., *Power Volleyball* (C.V.A. Publications, 1968).

Cherebetiu, Gabriel, *Volleyball Techniques* (Creative Sports Books, 1969).

Cohen, Harlan, *Power Volleyball Drills* (Creative Sports Books, 1967).

James, Dave, *Volleyball for Schools* (Pelham, 1976).

Keller, Val, *Point, Game and Match* (Creative Sports Books, 1968).

Keller, Val, *Coaching Supplement to Point, Game and Match* (Creative Sports Books).

Laveaga, Robert, *Volleyball* (A. S. Barnes & Co., 1942).

Nicholls, Keith, *Modern Volleyball: for teacher, coach and player* (Henry Kimpton, 1973).

Pankhurst, Roy (editor), *Volleyball* (Blacks).

Prsala, Jan, *Fundamental Volleyball Contacts* (C.V.A. Publications, 1971).

Scates, Allen E., *Winning Volleyball* (Allyn & Bacon, 1972).

Sortir, Nochola, *Winning Volleyball*, transl. J. D. Syer (Stanley Paul, 1973).

Wardale, P. R., *Volleyball: Skills & Tactics*.

Closing ceremony at Montreal Olympics. Japan, gold medal; Russia, silver medal; and, being presented, Korea, bronze medal